DEATH
IS ALL
ABOUT ME

D1714707

DEATH
IS ALL
ABOUT ME

How Being Near the Dying
Brought Me Closer to the Living

KELLY CARTER
MERRILL

Independently Published

Independently published in the United States.

Library of Congress Cataloging-in-Publication Data

Merrill, Kelly Carter.
Death is All About Me: How Being Closer to the Dying Brought Me Closer to the Living / Kelly Carter Merrill

ISBN 979-8-8517-6032-7 [pbk.]

Subjects
Nonfiction: Family & Relationships | Nonfiction: Death Grief, Bereavement | Nonfiction: Body, Mind, & Spirit | Nonfiction: Inspiration & Personal Growth

Keywords
1. Memoir 2. NICU 3. Academic Career 4. Motherhood 5. Marriage 6. Personal Growth 7. Spiritual Development

Locations
Virginia | Pennsylvania | Chicago | Honolulu | Taiwan

Cover design by Malia Wisch
Back cover photo by Diego Valdez
Newspaper clipping printed with permission by
The Free Lance-Star, Fredericksburg, VA, July 5, 1999

"Nothing ever goes away until it teaches us what we need to know."
— Pema Chödrön

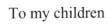

To my children

Table of Contents

Introduction ix

Chapter 1:   December 7, 2007 1

Chapter 2:   Chris...6

Chapter 3:   Maria...15

Chapter 4:   Shannon 27

Chapter 5:   Elizabeth 35

Chapter 6:   The Prophets Jeff and Nancy 45

Chapter 7:   Nick...51

Chapter 8:   Miriam 57

Chapter 9:   December 7, 2007 67

Chapter 10: Rebecca..72

Chapter 11: Peyton 78

Chapter 12: Career...89

Chapter 13: Liko..98

Chapter 14: Eliza 105

Chapter 15: Dr. Tai...112

Chapter 16: Dr. Jansen 117

Chapter 17: Labor...139

Chapter 18: Danny..149

Chapter 19: Grace...168

Chapter 20: Taiwan 178

Chapter 21: Journey..196

Epilogue..206

Acknowledgements 207

About the Author..209

All of these events are true, although I have changed the names
and some of the descriptions of
most of these people.

Introduction

Since the day I was born, death continues to be an awkward companion in my life. By the time I turned 40, ten of my peers had died, including childhood friends and neighbors, high school friends, college friends, a colleague, a boss, and *three* exes — two boyfriends and one girlfriend. I have one living ex-partner — the only one where I initiated the break-up. The secret to surviving a break-up with me seems to be, let me do it. My husband has been warned. A few of the deaths have been quick accidents (drowning, highway accident, country road accident), two were suicides, but most have known they were dying. Three of these people have died *on* my birthday — an infamous death day. I've observed three of my birthdays in mourning (24, 32, and 40); one of those was an ex. Two other birthdays I did not observe at all (18 and 19) — for other life-adventure reasons. More than once I've asked, *What is it with me and death? If death keeps showing up in my life, maybe it has something to teach me.*

I was born on December 7, 1971, the thirtieth anniversary of an infamous death day — Pearl Harbor Day. Franklin Delano Roosevelt called it a "date which will live in infamy"; I call it a birthday. On December 7, 1941, the Japanese Navy attacked the United States Navy in Hawai'i, killing nearly 2,500 soldiers and civilians alike. The attack spurred the United States' involvement in World War II, which in turn cost even more lives. So calling it a *birth*day seems a misnomer.

Even on the day I was born, my father was certain my mother and I had both died. In 1971 fathers weren't allowed into the delivery room. He waited in the designated fathers' lounge.

The other fathers joked that the first of them to have a girl should name her Pearl. An intercom voice congratulated Mr. Jones on the birth of his son and instructed him to step through the double doors to greet his family. His parting words were, "Well, Pearl will be one of yours," pointing to the other dads-to-be. Moments later, the intercom announced that Mr. Martin had a son as well, and he too disappeared behind the swinging doors. Then, "Mr. Carter, will you proceed through the double doors?" No congratulations. No "son" or "daughter" announcement. He panicked. A nurse silently greeted him and escorted him down a long hallway to the left. Finally, they pushed through a single swinging door to the right. Immediately behind that door was a gurney-type bed with a sheet pulled over two head-shaped lumps. After an intense initial sob, the nurse kindly pointed out that my father was grieving over my mother's covered feet. We were both fine at the opposite end of the gurney.

I've never had a brush with death myself, though many people close to me have. Besides those who have actually passed away, quite a few more family members and friends have come close but survived. Funny thing, you don't know if you're really dying until you're dead. My friends and family who survived breast cancer, meningitis, Leukemia, and heart attacks all faced death as if it were imminent. *Four* times in my life people in offices next door to mine have had cancer – three survived, one didn't. Of course it crossed my mind that perhaps something environmental was going on, and that I too was at risk. When I was 27, my father was technically dead for four minutes after a heart-attack while swimming, which led to his near-drowning. The heroic efforts of his friend, a CPR-certified scuba diver, brought him back.

Yes, deaths happen around many of us, for sure. For me, my experiences with peer deaths started happening when I was a young adult. The first death was a college suite-mate committing suicide when I was 19. The deaths continued with steady frequency — a frequency that shocked others whenever I started listing these experiences. Throughout my 40s, I realized that, as I get older, the deaths of people close to me will only increase in frequency. It just comes with "that" age. My father used to joke

The Free-Lance Star, July 5, 1999.

that his mother's conversation-starters were about her friends who had died recently. Now *he's* at that age. I'll likely never get a break from my proximity to death.

This book tells three interweaving stories. First, this is the story of my unlikely proximity to death — the story of death being all around me. There have been times when I've averaged one death a year, and other times when it would seem I've dodged the trend only to be reminded again that I can't. Death is all about me in that it always seems to surround me, but there's also something about *me* when it comes to death. Circumstances – like dates, dreams, and messages – seem to be telling me that these things have been happening for a reason, a personal message to me from the universe. I've wondered what lesson I'm supposed to reap from these connections with death, lest they continue happening. It took me years, and all of these experiences, to finally learn that I am dying too – we all are – and if there are any blessings in knowing that you are dying, they are available to all of us right now.

Second, this book tells the story of life lessons from death. I've had many conversations about life from the vantage point of death, with the people who know the subject best. Through these experiences I've become less shy about discussing what dying does to people's decisions, mental talk, and relationships. Those facing certain death have passed along wisdom that has proved invaluable, such as being able to discern valuable friendships, identifying and aligning personal priorities, learning the boundaries of our control, gaining awareness of our self-centering narratives, and knowing when to allow life to happen to us, rather than resist it. After having so many of these kinds of conversations with people on the brink of passing away, I've seen what emerges as the most important lessons.

Third, this is my own personal story of repeated personal loss, change, and new beginnings. If there is such a thing as a usual person, I'm not it. If anything, you could perhaps say that I'm a typical unusual person. I strive on some level to be like everybody else, to relate to the human condition in some common way like the folks around me. But my life's path has taken several less popular turns — changing religions, moving around the country, and engaging in various types of relationships. This is the story of my life's twists and turns through the lens of my experiences with loss in general, and with death in particular.

Chapter 1

December 7, 2007

O ne weekend in April of 2007, when I was 35, my fiancé
Dan and I were staying at his parents' home in Pittsburgh
while we made final arrangements for our wedding,
scheduled to take place there in one month. I got a phone call
from a high school friend letting me know that Brian, a high
school boyfriend of mine, had just taken his own life. I hadn't
kept in touch with Brian, so I had no idea why suicide would be
an option for him. Sara explained that he had been dealing with
drug addiction. Married, with two small children, he'd just had a
fight with his wife who had grown tired of hiding and
accommodating his illness. She gave him an ultimatum – "Tell
your parents or I will." Her motivation was not to punish him;
she just needed his parents' support to get him the help he
needed, and to get help herself as she tried to manage a
household with young kids and a needy drug addict. Brian was
stunned. He told her, "I need some time and space to deal with
your demands. Just let me think!" She took the kids out shopping
and left him alone in the house. He called her cell phone and said,
"I just want you to know that this is your fault," and he hung up.
She returned to the house *with the kids*, to find that he'd shot
himself in the head. At least this is how the story went.

Brian and I had grown up next door to each other. He had
moppy, sandy blonde hair and a thick but fit build. He had
double-jointed fingers that I found endearing. He was likely more
popular than me, but he was a year younger so that seemed to
even things out between us. For a brief seven-month window we

"dated" as high school kids without driver's licenses do. We'd sneak in and out of each other's houses and camp in each other's back yards. We made out a few times. We went to a homecoming dance together. Then that was about it; it was over just because it was over. There was no real break-up moment that I can remember. He just stopped talking to me one day. I think he'd lost interest, and I didn't mind, so I wrote him a letter agreeing that it was over and I moved on.

But on this day in April of 2007, my father still lived near Brian's parents. I called my father to ask him what he knew of Brian's life or death. He confirmed most of the story that Sara had told me, adding that he thought Brian's dad probably bought him the drugs.

I had to return to my fiancé and his family with this thought in my head. Another dead ex–*number three*. I was sad for Brian and his family, but I also felt stricken — as if I were at fault or at least I should examine my connection to Brian's tragic death. The timing felt odd — did this mean something? Did this mean that I shouldn't get married? Was I cursed? Did this mean my fiancé Dan would die too? Dan already knew about the first two. We decided that one was sad; two was coincidence. But *three*? I didn't know what to think of three. I told Dan that Brian had just died, well, because I always told him everything. He was surprised, but he followed my lead.

"These things just happen to me," I told him, "and then I move on. There is absolutely nothing that wallowing can do to change it. So, let's go on with things, shall we? Which flower arrangements do we like best? Yes, the wildflowers."

But late at night, when I couldn't sleep, my mind was occupied with thoughts of Brian, as well as my other exes who had died: Chris and Shannon.

By most accounts, the year 2007 was the best year of my life. I graduated with my doctorate in early May and was hired to a tenure-track faculty position at the University of Hawai'i. Later that same month, I married my best friend, Dan. In late July we moved to Honolulu, where months later we would conceive our first child. Moving to Honolulu also allowed me to finally explore a place that I hoped would add some clarity to my unusual connection with death.

Pearl Harbor, which was attacked on the date that would become my birthday, felt holy to me because it seemed to hold a key of some sort to all of the ways death had been following me around throughout my life. I felt drawn to journey there one day. I watched movies and documentaries about the 1941 Pearl Harbor attack. I obtained an obscure audio recording of Orson Welles's radio performance of *Between Americans*, which was originally broadcast the evening of December 7, 1941, after the news hit the mainland. The piece questioned what it meant to be American. What did it mean to rise up after decisive vulnerability? As my life progressed, this felt like my story too.

I was thrilled to move to Honolulu for many reasons, chief among them was the opportunity to not only visit Pearl Harbor, but to really spend quality time there. Instead of rushing to Pearl Harbor to experience the typical tourist experience, I wanted to save it for my birthday. And I wanted to do it alone. We moved to Honolulu in July, and I didn't approach Pearl Harbor or Pearl City until December 7, 2007. It was the 66th anniversary of the attack, and my 36th birthday.

I was two months pregnant. At the time, only my husband knew about the pregnancy. I woke up at 5 am and left the house by 5:30 to arrive in time to get tickets to the annual memorial service held across the harbor from the site of the attack. I wore black capri polyester stretchy pants, with a preggo waistband, and a thin, white, patterned embroidered aloha blouse. I brought a rain jacket and umbrella with me as all locals know to do. I arrived at the parking lot at the insanely early hour of 6 am. It was still dark. The event wouldn't start until nearly two hours later. I was among the very first there. I made it. I was in.

The strangest thing happened during the water taxi to the event venue. We all sat on benches packed in like sardines. My seat was on the end of a bench right next to the edge of the boat – a great spot for viewing the sights as we taxied across the harbor, past the memorial, and on to the event venue. I felt lucky, as if the universe knew it was my special day, even if the people around me didn't know. As the boat moved, I was taking everything in. Suddenly, I felt as though a bucket of water had been dumped on my head, thoroughly drenching me. A constant stream of water doused me the entire boat ride. Either the spray from the boat was somehow soaking us from overhead, which seemed like an unlikely angle, or else a sudden, torrential, tropical downpour was hitting us at precisely the same time that we taxied. From where I was sitting, I couldn't see where the water came from. Indeed closing my eyes seemed more reasonable than looking around. Others around me were also being drenched. No one moved or struggled to get dry. It occurred to me that I had a rain jacket in my bag, but it seemed entirely too late. So I just sat there and decided to enjoy it. After all, the universe knew it was my day, so it must have been a special spiritual cleansing of sorts. A baptism. I was soaking wet, thankful, and glowing.

We arrived at the venue and immediately the deluge stopped. When I stepped from the boat, I looked to the sky and saw a mostly blue sky with a few large white passing clouds. I wondered, *Could one of those have doused us?* But I didn't find the puzzle interesting enough to belabor; I moved on. My hair was soaked, but I was able to finger comb it to a reasonable style. I was thankful for polyester and thin aloha blouses, as I mostly dried out within an hour. The venue was a very large Naval supply pavilion that had been set up for the event. Imagine a carport that is large enough to hold three commercial jet airplanes. A few octogenarians greeted people as they got off the boat. They wore matching blue velvet garrison caps with golden piping. Yes, there would be veterans here today, probably survivors. Rows and rows of folding chairs were arranged facing a stage, the backdrop of which was the harbor; far away on the other side of the harbor, I could barely see the Pearl Harbor Memorial. It looked about the size of a small, solid, white rambler-style home. The ends of the roof slightly curved up. This structure was built over the sunken USS Arizona. So that's where it all happened. Here, 66 years ago, thousands of people were killed; thus turning what would 30 years later be my birthday into an infamous death day.

Along the stage were hundreds of flower arrangements, the type that you see at funerals – the kind that stand on easel legs, with wide ribbon banners across them labeling who they are for and from. Over the next hour, hundreds more people were shuttled in. We took our seats to ensure good spots, but we waited and waited. This was a perfect time for people watching. I felt completely satisfied that I had finally arrived. I felt special. *I'm at Pearl Harbor on my birthday.*

The program consisted of Hawai'i politicians, local news media personalities, military personnel, and historians. Speakers made reference to Tom Brokaw's speech the year before for the 65th anniversary. A military band played several patriotic songs. It all felt honorable, respectful, historical, and special. It was such an honor for me to be there that day. I anticipated that this would be my special place, but it was my first day there, so I took in as much as I could. I wanted it all to feel familiar as quickly as possible. *This place and I, we go way back.* The sounds of the band, the droves of tourists around me...the flower bouquets...Hawaiian breezes....

I sat by myself waiting for the ceremony to begin, still slightly damp all over. I did not have a particular life goal to end up in Hawai'i, and yet here I was. *Life led me here.* I felt that I was supposed to be here, so I opened my senses. I suspected a lesson would be here waiting for me. And it was, just moments away. Before the lesson would come, though, I reflected on my life experiences that brought me to this moment — my own experiences with loss, decisive defeat, and even the deaths of loved ones.

Chapter 2

Chris

Depending on how you count it, Chris and I dated for nearly two years. We met our junior year of high school in 1988 in a history class in our hometown in Central Virginia when we were both 16. He became my boyfriend on the very last week of that school year, but it was a huge risk for him.

Chris was a Jehovah's Witness and I had been raised Protestant. He wasn't even supposed to be my friend; as a non-JW, I was a "bad association." He wasn't even supposed to date at all, even if I had been a JW. JWs date in group settings with no alone time. Being my boyfriend didn't just risk disapproval by his family, but he risked outright "disfellowship" from his full extended family, friends, congregation, and anyone who he had ever been allowed to feel close to. He risked his whole world to be in love with me.

He was perfect — a sweet boy, with dark hair, blue eyes, fair skin, and slight freckles. He was tall and athletic. We were crazy about each other. Since there were other JWs at the school, we had to be discreet there. Instead of passing notes and risking being seen, we decided to share a plain spiral notebook; it was yellow. I wrote a love letter on the first few pages, then passed it on to him. He'd do the same and so on. We went through two entire spiral notebooks. We decided that he could never take them home, so I kept them. I held onto those notebooks for 20 years. They were so precious to me. In addition to the notebooks, I had made him a wooden lock box; we just called it "the box." I wanted him to have some things at his home to remember me by. It was the size of an index card box, and I screwed on a full-sized latch. Chris contributed a special combination lock for it that was gold. I still remember the combination 12-38-8. In the box were pictures of me and us, a pair of earrings that I wanted to wear on my wedding day, a mixtape, and other things I can't remember now.

It seemed popular media "got us" as we identified our story in movies and music. *Princess Bride* was our movie. The stable boy and the princess had a secret love affair as did we. The secret way that they said I love you in public was, "as you wish." We adopted that as well, and added the abbreviation AYW.

Occasionally, we did a very risky thing; we would both sneak out of our houses to meet up at midnight and stay together until 4am. I'd hop in my car and drive 30 minutes to his house and park at the end of his street in a dark area out of sight from any houses. He'd slide into the car and we'd cuddle and talk for hours. We talked about our darkest secrets, that time when an older woman sexually harassed him, and that time when my older neighbor felt me up. At that time there was no one in our lives that knew either of us better than each other.

We went on like this in utter secrecy our entire senior year. Being 16, madly in love for the first time in my life, and unable to tell the world was extremely challenging. I told only my parents and two of my friends of whom he approved, and they were sworn to secrecy. And that was it. I went to homecoming and prom with other boys as friends. I know I left those boys very confused. By the end of the year, Chris didn't care as much about hiding us. We went to a few graduation week activities together including a pool party event with many other members of our class. It was amazing to be seen with him – to be out – although we still didn't touch each other.

He knew we could be happier together than many married couples were. And I believed him. We talked deeply about what it might be like to be married, to have kids, to be a real public couple. He would work construction; I would be a teacher and we'd be so amazingly happy. Never mind the detail of our religious differences. We talked about him leaving the Witnesses, but that didn't seem likely. We talked of me joining, but that didn't seem likely either. We held hope that we could have it all, our own religions and each other.

The summer before I left for college, he wanted to tell his parents about us. He was tired of hiding, and he was pretty certain that we were going to get married. They took it well. His dad asked if he really loved me, and he did. His dad said that it would be a hard life, but they'd support him. They invited me over for dinner and we played a trivia game afterwards. His two younger brothers were away at their grandparents' house. I had to pretend that I'd never been in their house before — but I had. I wanted to be on my absolute best behavior. I made conscious efforts to be delightful, conversational, helpful, and asexual. I did make the mistake of knowing the answer to one of the trivia questions about a racy romance writer. After the dinner, they seemed to mildly approve. In retrospect, though, I think that they wanted to play along, so as to not push him away from them directly into my arms.

That fall I went to college at Virginia Tech and he made my send-off special — gifts to remember him by, including my own box. He came to visit me once with his friend Darius. He wanted to see my room, where I ate and slept. He wanted to meet people and know my world as best he could. He was afraid of the distance, of us drifting. As far as I was concerned, he had nothing to worry about. He was my everything.

We tried to talk on the phone every Friday, but long-distance phone bills were a disabling reality in 1989. Conversations were brief when they did happen. We wrote each other letters. I wrote him exactly two.

I worried about sending Chris letters. It was a bold move. If he wasn't the one home to get the mail, his parents or younger brothers would see it. Having my letter in their hands felt like flaunting — putting them in a position to pass on my love notes. I sent the first letter and it arrived safely in Chris's possession. It was banal. "Hi. How are you? I miss you. College is cool. I'm meeting nice friends. Classes are okay. I dropped calculus." I wanted it to be informative to him, yet safe in case it was intercepted. During one of our Friday talks I was interested to hear if he'd received it. He had. He explained that he's usually the first one home. *Ah good.*

I wanted to quell Chris's concerns about our distance. I wanted to send him a juicy letter, as we used to do with the notebook. I wanted him to be excited to see me again. At college, I was in a position to be more in control of myself and my decisions. I decided that I wanted to get on birth control pills. In my next letter I explained to Chris that I had just started taking them, and in about two months I would be safe. By our next Friday phone call he should have received my letter, but he hadn't. It was a mystery. I asked if it was possible that his parents had it. Maybe, but not likely. I ended up telling him what I had written. We agreed that it would be utterly horrible if they saw that letter. He agreed to make a point to be the first to the mailbox until it arrived.

Two days later, on a Sunday morning in October 1989, Chris called my room. I was thrilled, yet surprised since every good Witness would be at the Kingdom Hall on a Sunday morning.

"I had a very rough day yesterday, Kelly. I'm home alone right now. The rest of my family is at the Kingdom Hall; they agreed to leave me home today to call you. They are even paying the phone bill." Pause. "My parents *did* get that letter." Long pause. "We have to break up. There's no future for us."

"That's your parents talking."

"But they are right. Where did we really think this was going? I've gotten so far off track. I've strayed from the Truth. I've done things I'm not proud of."

"Because you love me." I was sobbing.

"I love Jehovah. That has to come first. I haven't been who I want to be, who I was before knowing you."

"We've always said that love is all that matters. That we'll find a way, as long as we love each other."

"I do love you, but I've got to get over that. It's just not going to work."

"I can look into converting. No promises, but I will seriously look into it."

"You can't do that any more than I can."

"I haven't tried yet. I think you did give it a try, but I haven't at all. Let me give it a try. Let me learn more about it."

"I can't teach you."

"I know."

"It has to be for you, not for me."

"It would have to be. I couldn't do it just for you. You'd leave me for your beliefs, so they must be pretty special. I should give it a chance. I'll look into it."

"But, I can't even talk to you. We can't write or talk or visit anymore." More crying from him.

"I can't believe this is happening. This feels so unreal. We're both so in love. Why would people in love break up? Why is this happening? That dumb letter. This wouldn't be happening if it wasn't for my dumb letter."

"No, but it's good. The longer we went on like this, the harder this would be later."

"This can't be harder, Chris. This is the worst." At this point I was sobbing. "I can't hang up with you."

"We don't have to for a while. My family will be gone for another hour. We can stay on the phone until then."

"I'd like that. I just want to hear your voice as long as I can, even your breathing." Breathing. "But what can we even talk about? How you want to leave me, even though you love me?!"

"I just can't talk to you, or communicate with you. So, yeah, it makes sense to break up."

"Let's *not* say that we're breaking up, then. If we both love each other and have each other's hearts, what does it matter that we don't communicate? People have done that, right? Prisoners? Believe in me, Chris. The next time you hear from me, I'll be baptized."

Eventually we did hang up to many tears and sobs on both sides of the phone. If this conversation would count as our break-up, then our relationship lasted 16 months. I was a wreck for weeks. I didn't leave my room for three days. My roommate was reasonably worried about me. I couldn't talk to her without crying so hard that my sobs stole my words. She snuck food out of the dining hall for me.

To get out of my funk I took control of my situation the only way I could. I called the local Kingdom Hall. This was the only chance at getting my wonderful life back the way it was.

I studied weekly one-on-one with my own private Pioneer. My assigned Pioneer's husband was an elder and they had two high school daughters. One was trying her best to drift from the family due to her worldly interests (read: probably a boyfriend); the other, Anne, became my friend. In addition to my weekly private sessions, I went to the standard set of JW meetings — three per week. Each of these meetings required preparation. JWs read their Bibles before meetings and prepared answers to study questions. I found this impressive. Every one of them studies the Bible since it is part of the regular meetings. On top of this, I was a college student, granted just an average one, with these other JW commitments. I didn't mind as the studies felt like a worthy use of my time. I was attracted to the clarity and certainty of their Biblically-based beliefs – which they affectionally call The Truth.

I knew that by summer break, I'd be back in my hometown, and likely to see Chris again since I'd need to connect to a Kingdom Hall. I'm sure he knew that it would be likely. The Kingdom Hall for my living area was not the same as Chris's, so I didn't see him immediately. I found a new Pioneer for the summer break, and she had a lovely family. Her husband was an elder and their two girls were middle school aged. They looked up to me, which I was uncomfortable with. I didn't want to hurt them, and I just might. I suppose on some level I worried that this religion thing wouldn't work out. But, I became close to them that summer, as I felt compelled to distance myself from my own non-Witness family.

After being in my hometown for several weeks, I became closer to some of the JW youth who were my age. I hadn't told anyone about Chris. I didn't want to defend my intentions. But one day the older youths planned a get-together with others from Chris's congregation.

Chris and I talked. It seemed natural. It was absent of flirting, or maybe just a touch. It felt mature to me. "How's your mom doing? How does Alex like high school? Where have you been working? How do you like it?" I learned that he had been doing more pioneering work in addition to his time at the local power company, but he otherwise kept his distance from me.

I talked to my friend Gizela about it, and she mentioned softly that maybe he wasn't into me. I dismissed her; I thought she didn't fully understand my history with him. And I understood his need to keep a safe distance.

"Actually, have you seen how he looks at Nadia? I think he likes her." Nadia was Gizela's younger sister.

"Really? No I hadn't. Are they already a thing, and I'm too blind to see it?"

"Not that I know of." But I didn't believe her. She knew.

The next chance I got, I pulled Chris's friend Darius to the side. "Is this true? Is Chris interested in Nadia?"

"Kelly, you have to understand. He got over you. He was really torn up for about two months. Finally we got him to a camp with a big ol' bonfire. He brought any memorabilia he had of yours. Pictures, letters, it all went into the fire. Like a band-aid. He had to. He was too miserable to keep living like that. The final step was helping him to find someone new to focus on. Nadia's family had just moved into town and they've been JWs for several generations, just like his."

I had no choice but to confront Chris before the gathering ended.

"I heard from both Gizela and Darius that you might be interested in Nadia. Is this true?"

"Well..." Shrug.

"Look it's okay. I'm not angry. It makes sense. I just want to know so I can stop thinking about you." I had a tear in one eye and my chin quivered. *Oh great, I'm cracking. He can't see me like this.*

"Well, yeah, I guess it's true."

My last words to him ever were, "Okay then. As you wish." And I walked away. I went to the restroom, brushed off my tears and washed my face. I cooled off. I wanted him to see me doing wonderfully, despite the news. I came back out, avoided eye contact with him, and chatted with the gals, including Gizela and her sister, Nadia. I was delightful and polite.

I said complimentary things. I excused myself, left, and never went back to that Kingdom Hall again.

I had no idea that I had already said goodbye to him for the last time ever. I would never see Chris again, and in a few years his passing would become another important milestone in my unusual journey alongside death.

To me, this was the day we had really broken up — a few months after the two-year mark of first calling him my boyfriend. This break-up didn't hurt nearly as much as the one nine months earlier over the phone; it would be easier to move on after this one. But how, I didn't know.

I had genuinely believed that JW might be the religion for me, so I wanted to come clean. I told my Pioneer in my hometown about my secret and what had happened with Chris. She was disappointed that I hadn't been honest with any of them earlier, but she promised to stick with me. I kept studying with her and limited my socializing to only with her family. I wanted to have nothing to do with the JW youth in my hometown. They felt like distractions.

I went back to college for my sophomore year in the fall of 1990 and continued studying there with JWs for one more semester.

But as the months continued, the religion couldn't hold me. My Pioneer's husband, the elder, left her and their daughters without a trace. Poof. Gone. They think he fled to the next state with a woman he met with some new-fangled technology called electronic mail. My Catholic roommate was a particularly "good association" for being a non-Witness — a much cleaner Christian than I. And my college peer resident assistant (RA), Maria, was a good association, too. She knew the Bible inside and out and could challenge me Biblically in ways that no other Protestant had. Her intelligence and logic were intoxicating.

I left the Witnesses after the Truth started to fall apart. I already knew that gays aren't bad, that non-Witnesses are not all "bad associations," that some Witnesses are, and that the Bible *does* contradict itself. The dualistic clarity that was initially appealing couldn't stand up to real-world complexity. I learned that life and religion aren't that certain. I knew leaving the

Witnesses would mean that Chris and I had no hope, but it seemed that that would be true even if I had stayed.

Since Christmas was coming, I didn't want it to seem that I'd changed my mind for the gifts or for the holiday spirit, as JWs don't celebrate Christmas. I waited until after I was back at school in January to cut my ties with the Witnesses. My roommate was thrilled for me.

It was hard to do. Our room received phone calls, five to ten per day, all Witnesses trying to talk me out of leaving. Elders, pioneers, youth from both the college town and hometown congregations. After I took the first two calls from an elder and my local Pioneer, I just couldn't take any more calls. I couldn't say the same thing over and over again to people who wouldn't accept it. I couldn't continue to be challenged by these people who knew every comeback in the book. I had to go cold turkey. There would be no answering phones for my roommate or me for a couple weeks. I was done. A part of my life had died when Chris and I parted ways and when the beliefs of JWs fell apart. When it came time to say goodbye to the JW religion, I had a much easier time handling that loss.

Due to the studying and time demands of the JWs, and their disapproval of worldly things like education and community involvements, my full college experience had been delayed. For the first year and a half at college, I wasn't involved in anything — no clubs, no intramural sports, no social groups beyond my immediate neighbors. When I placed the Witnesses and their judgments about my priorities behind me, I broke out of my confines and discovered campus life.

I pretty much left all religion. I claimed that I was "spiritual, but not religious" — but that was a lie. I paid minimal attention to my spiritual life for the next two decades.

Chapter 3

Maria

At the beginning of my sophomore year of college, I had a new RA who was fascinating to me. She was an international student from Indonesia. I didn't know a single thing about Indonesia, not even where it was. *Maybe near India?* I guessed that from the name. My relationship with Maria would open my perspectives on the world, religion, and even, well, me. By the end of the year, who I thought I was would be so dramatically shifted, that I'd come to mourn who I thought I was.

On move-in day, my roommate Isabel knew what to expect of me. She was a good Catholic, and I was a good Jehovah's Witness. Well…as far as she was concerned I was a Jehovah's Witness. I hadn't been baptized yet, though that was the goal. Over the summer we had decided on a color scheme for our dorm room and purchased coordinating comforters and sheets. I brought in my large low lounging chairs and my TV. She brought in the mini-fridge and color coordinated rug. We were excited for our room to look mature for the sophomores that we were.

"Hey Kelly! Good to see you."

"Hey, Izzy. How was your summer?"

"Pretty good."

"Did you get to spend much time with Paul?"

"Yeah, he worked a lot, but we got to hang out some."
And she rolled her eyes to the side.

"I hear ya. Good to see you. Hey, do you know when the RA meeting is? I need to tell my folks so they can leave then."

"Yeah, after dinner so you can go out and eat with your folks and just come back for that. That's what we're doing."

"Did you meet the RA? What's she like?"

"Yeah, she came by. She's sweet."

"Sweet?" I wondered what that meant.

"Yeah, not at all like our senior-itis RA last year who we never saw. She's friendly."

"You didn't think Lisa was friendly?" I thought she was.

"Well, I didn't really see her much, so there's that," Isabel continued to unpack.

"Right, and I had heard that she was a lesbian," I wondered if I knew something Isabel didn't.

"Yeah, I had heard that too, so maybe she hung out with that crowd."

I agreed. I pictured "that crowd" kind of being the social rejects. The fringe people with a half-way punk style and just socially awkward. I wasn't really interested in knowing them anyway.

"So I hope that her kindness is a good thing," I could see a kind RA not being able to keep our hallway quiet on study nights.

"I think so."

"What's her name?"

"Oh, I don't know. She said it, but...I don't remember. She's...um...she's Asian."

"Oh, okay." And I assumed it was some international name that I would find difficult to remember, much less pronounce. "Well, I'll see you tonight at the meeting." And I was out.

Later that night at the RA meeting, I walked in a bit late to a crowded hallway lounge. All fifty of us tried to squeeze into a room the size of a UHaul. Some were lucky to be sitting in the soft chairs and couches that furnished the room, but the rest of us sat on the floor, some snuggled together and braided hair. Others stood against the back wall. I made my way into the center of the room to sit on the floor by my roommate. I scanned the room for the freshmen. They stood out with scared eyes.

Through the tight crowd of my new neighbors, our RA stood small and humble. She looked super cute in her oversized

Residence Life-issued polo shirt tucked into her khaki shorts, bright white socks and shoes. She was thin and tan, a standard bob haircut with bangs and coarse jet black hair. Her eyes were deep brown as she scanned the room to look directly at each one of us.

The RA tried to speak, but it was difficult to command attention in that room, especially with her soft voice. We helped her out by yelling out louder. "Hey, y'all, pay attention!"

"Hi everyone. Welcome. My name is Maria, like in the *Sound of Music.*"

Oh, I see, not an unusual name, but rather a common one. I can remember that.

"I'm a senior majoring in chemistry."

Oh boy, another senior. We're never going to see her, especially with that chem major. She's going to be too kind. Are the trouble-makers going to walk all over her? I don't want a loud floor.

She asked us what we hoped for our community.

I spoke up, "I hope we can all get to know each other. And consider each other good neighbors."

"Good. Thanks for sharing. I hope for that, too. Others?" Maria was encouraging.

A junior spoke up, "That sounds nice and all, but I really want to get work done. I was off campus last year in an apartment and had noisy neighbors and no RA to help out, so I'm back on campus this year hoping for a more studious place."

"That's a great point, too. Thanks for sharing that." Maria nodded.

As the meeting went on, I could sense that Maria had an accent. She told us of upcoming "manDATory" meetings to put on our "calANDers," putting her emphasis on the second syllable.

Where is she from?

She didn't seem like the Vietnamese refugee kids I went to high school with. And, really, at that point in my life, that was it for my exposure to anyone with Asian ancestry.

As the weeks went on, Maria proved to be a good RA, walking through the halls to meet us and make conversation.

When she stopped by our room, Izzy and I were excited to show her our room decor. We had our loft bed set up to the right with the lounge chairs and TV underneath. The "kitchen area" with mini-fridge was to the left. Straight ahead were our two closets and two desks against the wall. As a sophomore, I felt like kind of a big deal. Last year at this time I had been intimidated by my RA, this year she felt like friend potential.

Izzy and I went to see her room. It was clean and sparse, only the essentials. Her bed was low on the floor against the window. In addition to the two built-in desks against the wall she had a large desk that she had made with a door and two filing cabinets against the opposite wall. No posters, no rug, one hanging towel. Her bedspread was a fancy cloth with intricate designs and colors.

"Nice room. Very simple. You travel light. Where are you from?"

She looked up at her bangs with an uncomfortable smile. "I'm from Richmond."

I laughed and smiled, "Richmond? That's not a Richmond accent."

"I went to high school in Richmond."

"But where are you from, from?"

She exhaled. I wondered why this was hard.

"You asked where I'm from. I'm from Richmond."

"No, I mean...maybe your family? Your ancestry? Your origins? You know what I mean. ... You have an accent."

"Right, yes." She seemed to reluctantly concede, "I grew up in Indonesia. My father went to graduate school in Richmond, so I went to high school and college while he was there."

"Where is he now?"

"He graduated. My parents are back in Indonesia now."

Whoa. "So you up and moved countries in high school? Wow!"

"Yes my sinlings, too."

"How did you learn English?"

She laughed at me, "In Indonesia, in school, since I was 5!"

"Oh wow. Did you know it well enough to catch on immediately in Richmond?"

"More or less. I guess enough to know what was happening in academics. Friends were harder, but that became easier with time."

This was fascinating to me. I had never met anyone like Maria, and she was so easy to talk to.

"So where is Indonesia? I honestly have no idea."

Over the next few months I continued to learn about Indonesia's geography, government, economy, and socio-historical climate. I learned that Maria's father was a Christian minister with a PhD, and an author of several books for the Christian community in Indonesia. I learned that Indonesia is a Muslim country, so his ministry was not wholly welcomed. Maria was named to indicated her family's religion, a Christian name. I learned that Maria and her family didn't look like typical Indonesians, because they are ethnically Chinese and a small ethnic minority in Indonesia. I learned that Maria's Chinese ancestors had been in Indonesia longer than my European ancestors had been in the US. Between being Christian and ethnically Chinese, her family was marginalized in Indonesia. I learned the derogatory name that folks like her are called, that she had been called in public as she moved through her crowded hometown of Jakarta — "Cheena." When she told me, she hung her head low, and I knew to never repeat that word.

Maria's parents sent her handwritten airmail letters regularly. I enjoyed when she offered to read them to me. The letters were written mostly in English with some Indonesian sentences. Once they sent a newspaper clipping, an article about her father's work and his newest book. She translated it for me. On the backside were help-wanted ads for jobs. I asked her to read those to me.

"See, here's what I mean about the discrimination in Indonesia." She showed me an ad for a secretarial position. "Only attractive young women apply, no Cheena."

"Oh wow, right there in the ad! Not an unspoken thing, but right there in the ad!"

"Yes, so not like the US at all. You'd never see that in the US."

"Well, I imagine that an ad might have looked like that in the US in the 1950s, before it became illegal."

"Right, so in some ways that's where Indonesia is right now, 1950s-USA."

"Do you ever want to go back?"

"Not really."

"But how could you stay?"

"I hope to get a job here that will sponsor me. That's probably the most likely. But my brother and sister and I all enter the green card lottery every year, too."

"What's that?"

"The US draws names every year of people who get a green card just for having their names pulled."

"Really?! That's crazy. I mean such a personal thing up to a lottery?"

"Well, what else are they going to do? Everyone has a compelling story. And I think there are probably avenues for folks with the most compelling of stories. It's just this program the US runs, and it's a shot for us to maybe stay. And I guess there's a chance that I could get married, too."

We talked about her love life, which was non-existent at that point. I asked about living so far from her family. And if they wanted to return here. I asked about her worries of having to leave. We talked and talked and talked. After getting to know each other better, it seemed that we talked only to each other.

Maria was a good person, by any standard. Where I had sinned with alcohol, smoking, and general hedonism, she had not. She was a preacher's kid — the good kind. She knew her Bible, and I respected that. As a recovering Jehovah's Witness, I enjoyed being taken to task by a Christian who likely knew more about the Bible than I did. I loved hearing about her culture — learning from her first-hand experiences. I loved learning from her; I felt I was becoming a better person. Her skin was smooth, and I felt content as we snuggled next to each other for long chats. I took her home to my family for breaks. I became pen pals with her parents. We went on adventures together, and soon the people around us began to notice that we may be something more than just two good friends.

Izzy eventually commented, "You two are attached at the hip, aren't you?"

"I guess. We're good friends." But I hadn't thought of it in that way. *Attached at the hip? Are you saying that we spend too much time together? Am I neglecting you, my friend?*

So I tried to be more mindful of spending time with Izzy and began hiding how much time I spent with Maria. I would sneak to her room and not let Izzy know where I was. My talks with Maria would go later and later into the night, so much so that sometimes I'd spend the night. I would sneak out of her room very early the next morning before others were up, hoping that no one saw me through their peep hole.

Izzy noticed, "Um, Kelly, where were you?"

"Oh, I was at Maria's up late talking, so late that I just fell asleep there."

"But she only has one bed."

"Yeah, we both fit."

"Well," she clearly didn't believe me, "people are talking."

"Saying what?"

"What do you think they are saying when you sneak around like that? And stay overnight in her room?"

"Oh," and then it clicked. "OH! Really?!" *Oh my God, they think we're gay and doing stuff!* The thought had never occurred to me. "But who would say that? Who saw?" I wondered out loud.

"It doesn't matter. People are noticing. And they are talking."

"Is it you? Are you talking? Are you wondering? You could ask me, you know?!"

"No, it's not me. Others have asked me, and I honestly don't know what to say."

"But, Izzy, it isn't true. I mean do you even know me?! Do you know her? I mean, seriously, Maria?! Her?!"

"I know; that's what I tell them."

"But you have your doubts."

She looked at me from under her bangs. "Well, what *is* going on?"

"We're just really close friends. And, well, I guess we figured that people wouldn't understand. And that friends....okay...you...were feeling left out, so we got more sneaky. Seriously, we're just good friends."

"Okay, well, that's what I thought. But it does seem like more than that. I mean you could try to hang out with other people."

I knew I had to try. Both of our reputations were at stake.

"Yes, but now I have to tell her that this is going on. I mean, she's the RA, so it's a bigger deal for her than for me. What if the rumor gets to her boss? I'll have to tell her today after we're out of class. So you know I have to do that, right? I mean, I hear you that I need to keep my distance, but she needs to know this."

"Sure."

"She's going to be crushed. She's going to freak out."

"Yeah, okay. Just tell her this afternoon, but then come to dinner with us tonight in the dining hall, okay? You need to branch out your friendships."

"Okay."

"And let her have her own life."

"Right. Okay."

But I knew I was Maria's life. Who would she eat with? This rumor was ruining everything.

Later that night I went to Maria's room and told her the news.

"But it's not true!" She was crushed.

"I know."

"Why would they say that?"

"Because we were sneaking around."

"When do we sneak?"

"When we get on your bed and lock the door. When I spend the night."

"But they wouldn't understand that. It looks like something it's not." She rationalized.

"What wouldn't they understand, though?"

"Well, if they walked in, they'd see us in bed and think the things they are thinking. And they are wrong."

"Maria, they think we're very close. Is that wrong? Are we not close?"

"Well, we're not close in that way."

"In what way, though?" I wondered how she was making sense of this, as I was starting to see things from our neighbors' perspective.

"Nothing gay is going on!" she replied.

"But what is 'gay'?" I asked. "Isn't gay just loving someone of the same sex? Maybe we are. I've been thinking. Maybe we lock the door and sneak because deep down, we know it is not a normal friendship. We are very close."

"But not *that* kind of close," she cut in.

"Just because it's not physical, you mean?"

"Right. We don't do that," Maria countered.

"But we do lie down together in bed. Isn't that physical?"

"Oh, Kelly, you know what I mean! We are not gay!"

"I know what you mean. But I'm starting to wonder; I know what we do is not a normal friendship. We both knew that enough to try to hide it."

"Well, I think we just shouldn't spend the night together anymore."

"Agreed. And Izzy thinks I shouldn't spend as much time with you in general. Actually, I'm supposed to meet her for dinner soon, without you."

Maria looked at the floor in silence.

"I'm sorry. I want to be with you, but I don't want to hurt your reputation. I mean, you're the RA. People should feel able to approach you. And right now I take up all of your social time."

"But they are always welcome."

"Not with me around. You are more difficult to approach when I'm always around, especially if they are going to assume that I'm significant to you. You need to be a good RA. Go find some other residents to eat with tonight."

As she continued to stare at the floor, I noticed a tear creeping out of her eye. It crushed me. I reached out and hugged her. She was so soft.

"See? This is what I mean. The mere thought of not having dinner together feels this bad. I think you might love me. I mean, I think we love each other."

"I just feel so alone."

"Me too, but we're not. We are both surrounded by good people. Let's go meet them." This was easy for me to say; making close friends had never been hard for me.

We did go our separate ways. But that first night apart proved to be too tough for both of us to sustain. Within the week we were back to our old habits of spending the night together, sneaking but more stealthily, and becoming even closer. Perhaps the rumor pointed to what we did not yet know.

Through the rest of my sophomore year, we continued this way — not naming anything, just being close friends who sneak to hide how close we are. Nothing was ever more physical than lying next to each other in bed and sharing some hugs. I felt stuck between letting go of my old view of myself before Maria and this new possibility of loving another woman. As I was reckoning with which part of myself to let go of, I also began to notice my own mortality and the mortality of others around me.

By my junior year, I began to notice what I called a "death trend." Just in the first few weeks of the fall term I listed the following deaths in my journal: a high school friend of my roommate died of alcohol poisoning, the mother of our dorm's head RA died, my grandfather died, and even my dorm plant and three of the fish in our fish tank died. Then a tragedy struck for my group of friends from my freshman-year dorm — the first time I would experience a peer death. With the preceding peripheral deaths, I was primed to grieve. The news struck me hard and reminded me just how fragile my own mortality can be. I took notice.

September 26, 1991 Journal Entry
The day my grandfather died, Jessica (a suite-mate from freshman year) took two bottles of anti-depressants and then proceeded to get drunk. The two don't mix and she knew it. That Saturday night, she went into a coma. I heard the news from a fellow suite-mate. After I got over the initial shock, I wondered if she would ever try it again, assuming that this time her suicide attempt was not successful. Everyone knew why

she did it. Her parents were controlling her entitled life, all the while keeping their distance. Her freshman year they cut her $400 a month allowance when they learned of her many (seven) parking tickets. In her sophomore year she was pulled out during Fall semester, because she had gotten a DUI. And this junior year, she had gotten yet another DUI, so her parents wanted her to transfer to Texas Tech to be closer to her relatives so they, not her parents, could keep an eye on her. They should have obviously realized that their methods of parental-distancing discipline were not effective, and in reality, were causing more problems. Jessica was in a coma for a little less than a week. After she gained consciousness, she wrote a note to her mother, "Sorry, I love you." She swelled, her lungs collapsed and she died. My roommate was the one to tell me. I was shocked. I truly thought that she was going to recover. Apparently, she had been attempting suicide for a while. Her parents knew she was suicidal, but they didn't get her any help. They just kept punishing her and distancing her from them.

It's scary to know that it is possible to really screw up at parenting. I hope I am a good mother. It amazes me that some people are given life and don't want it. They'll do anything to get rid of it. Some people will do anything to hang on to their life when it is slowly being taken away by nature or another cause. What if they swapped lives?

These days, I look back on Jessica's life and death with a little more nuance than I did then. Maybe her parents didn't really screw up. Maybe they were trying their best, but were running out of options. Maybe Jessica needed more help than they could find. Maybe Jessica ran out of ways to ask for help.

Maria had begun a graduate program at our school, so she stayed on campus and we continued our relationship as usual. Maria continued to maintain that she was not gay, that she did love me, but not in that way. I questioned my sexual identity more and more. I knew that I had been in love with Chris, so if my love for Maria was real, then at the most I figured I was bisexual. Throughout my junior year I tried to distance myself from Maria by dating college men. I rationalized that if I were bisexual, then I could just turn off this part of me that loved Maria if I could only find the right guy. Then I'd have a chance at a normal life.

The boyfriends just weren't working out. I wasn't falling for them because I already had feelings for Maria. I missed her too badly when I was with them, and I loved being with her. My heart broke when I thought of how lonely she was when I was away.

By senior year, I was pretty convinced that I was probably gay. I didn't spend too much time trying to figure out my exact identity, or what caused me to be that way. I only told a handful of people and swore them to secrecy. All I knew was that I loved Maria, and she didn't love me the same way. I knew I had to move on, but that would have to wait until after graduation. As long as Maria was in my daily life, she had my heart whether she wanted it or not.

In college, I had lost any sense of spirituality that I may have had. I also lost my bearing on who I thought I was, no longer a heterosexual person. Twice now I had to move on from someone whom I loved and who loved me back. Turns out death does this too, makes us say good-bye forever to people we love and who love us back. This was training.

Chapter 4

Shannon

After graduation, I moved to Penn State for graduate school, where I felt free to shed secrets and pretenses. While I stayed in touch via long distance with Maria, in my new community, I was keen on finding others who were gay and lesbian. I came out from the start. I wanted to be called *gay* because I had too many prejudices attached to the word "lesbian" at that age. And bisexual, though it would have been more accurate, had no functional utility for me — which in the end meant that I had too many assumptions about that word as well. In my mind, bisexuals were non-monogamous, not committed, and insatiable; and that just wasn't me. I didn't spend energy hiding my sexual orientation, but I was also careful that it was not among the very first things that someone would know about me. I wanted new people to have an impression of me first without that knowledge, so that when they did learn, they would be able to distinguish the source of their prejudices of me. I felt free.

Within four months of living in my new community, I met Shannon. We met at a gay bar that I went to weekly. She was dancing, and I was watching. Shannon had chin-length dirty blonde hair, with a growing-out perm. Her body was fit, with clear muscle definition on her tan arms. She had rhythm and could dance. I asked my friends about her, and they knew of her. I learned that it took a while for us to meet in this small gay community because she had been in a controlling relationship for the past several months. Her partner wouldn't let her out or allow her to have friends. On the night we met, Shannon was celebrating her break-up. She was flattered by my interest, but initially the interest wasn't mutual. Too soon.

We began our relationship with long phone calls aimed at getting to know each other — what we enjoyed doing, what we valued, and who we were. Shannon was active in Judo and was working towards the next higher belt. She had been a camp counselor, and in high school, she had studied abroad in Brazil. She spoke Portuguese fluently. In my book, she was an intellectual rock star. The more I learned, the more I became drawn to her, and the feeling became mutual. I noticed a trend, *I am attracted to people who make me think.*

She was a sincere and caring person, and I admired her integrity. She wanted to become a recreational therapist. She worked well with people who had disabilities. One day I went to work with her at an independent living facility for adults with severe and profound disabilities. I was uncomfortable, but she was at home with them. Several didn't talk; some didn't walk. A few drooled constantly. A few residents needed her to feed them; others needed her to change their diapers. Some threw toddler-type tantrums but with their adult-sized bodies. It could have posed a danger for Shannon, yet she even enjoyed them, even taking out a few residents at a time for public trips, like to restaurants and shopping malls. She would tell me stories about the reaction others had, such as, "You shouldn't bring people like that out in public." I had no idea people would say things like that. But Shannon's stories made me aware that I too had been thinking similar things, and her stories challenged me on it. Shannon was good at her job and very smart about larger social issues involved in her work and in the lives of those she helped. She taught me about the disability rights movement. She moved me. Within a couple of months of dating, she moved in with me.

One evening, when I made dinner for Shannon, she delighted in telling me that she was pretty sure I was the first healthy relationship she had had. She had a high school boyfriend who raped her. Her most recent relationship was with a very controlling and manipulative woman. She even shared that her father had been physically abusive, burning and hitting her throughout her childhood. He had become good at hitting her where bruises would not be seen by others. This is why her parents were divorced. Her mom left him for the safety of Shannon and her sister. "Oh, Shannon, I'm so sorry that happened. I'm so happy to be in this relationship with you. You deserve a healthy life."

We had only been dating about four months when one night Shannon aggressively punched and kicked me as she slept. She apologized and turned to face the other way. We both fell back asleep. I didn't think much of it. The whole next day she was aloof and short with me; quick to anger. By the afternoon, I was getting irritated and confronted her.

"WHAT is going *on* with you?" I snapped at her.

"What makes you think it's me?"

"Oh, you think *I'm* triggering you? I'm just trying to get through this day, but I seem to keep irritating you at every turn. It's certainly not on purpose."

"You *could* ask me what's on my mind."

"That's what, '*What's going on with you?*' means!"

"Pff. Right. Like you care if something is bothering me."

Wait, what? I changed moods quickly. I calmed down and studied her eyes. Softly now, "Something *is* bothering you?"

"Obviously."

"Yes, can you tell me about it?"

"I wished you had asked me earlier this morning."

"I'm sorry I missed it. I'm asking now. What's on your mind? Is it me? Did I do something wrong?"

"No, not you."

"Then what?"

"It's very difficult, Kelly."

"I can see that. Is it serious?"

"Yes."

"Do you want to break up?"

"Oh my God, Kelly, not everything is about you, okay?!"

"I don't know what to say. I keep getting this wrong, and you don't seem to want to help me. Just tell me."

"Ugh. I had a bad dream last night. Okay?!"

"Okay, right. That's when you punched me."

"Right. It was a nightmare, Kelly."

"Obviously, if it's stuck with you this long into the day."

"Well, I've been thinking more about it, and I don't think it was just a dream. I think it was a memory."

"Whoa. Of what?"

"Remember I told you of the time my dad asked me to take off my glasses before he hit my face?"

"Yes, of course. That was awful. You are more valuable than glasses. He's a jerk."

"Right, well, I dreamt of that moment and what happened after he hit me."

"What happened after he hit you?"

"He raped me." She couldn't look at me. I couldn't not look at her. I rubbed her back. I wanted to hug her, but she looked like she didn't want to be touched.

"I'm so sorry. That's…that's horrible, Shannon. Do you think it really happened?"

"I don't know. But it's a horrible image to have in my head. Many of the details from the dream I know are memories. The glasses, the very frames that I know I had. The way he asked me to take them off. The way he carefully slugged my face. All of the other details were memories. Maybe that part is, too."

Shannon soon found an excellent counselor named Linda. They talked about the dream and did some detective work. Linda said it very likely was a memory. Being in a healthy relationship for the first time meant that Shannon wasn't living in survival mode any more. Emotionally, she was available to remember more abuse. When she was younger, Shannon had dissociated during the rape, meaning that she instantly forgot about it. She would essentially leave her body, because she just didn't have the level of emotional maturity to survive in that moment with her consciousness about her. It made sense.

The nightmares involving the same incident with the glasses continued every night. The scene would start earlier and then go later, until she had a fuller memory of what had happened that day. It was in her parents' bedroom. Her father wanted to discipline her for some type of typical kid misbehavior. He was fuming with anger. He locked the two of them together inside his room. He asked her to remove her glasses. She was afraid to, because she knew what it meant. He knew how to hit so that it wouldn't leave a mark. He walloped her face with an open hand.

She felt the stinging instantly. He was still raging with anger. Someone knocked on the door. Quietly at first, then harder and more panicked. He raped her right on the bed, on her mom's side, to the sound of her mother beating the door.

Then nightmares of other incidents joined the rotation. Her father often worked a night shift, came home at 2 a.m., went straight to her room, and woke her up to rape her in her own bed. Then she went back to sleep. That was the more usual scenario. Later she'd have nightmares of an old shed in the woods behind her house, but either she never got to see what happened inside, or she couldn't bear to tell me. She had no waking memory of such a shed existing at all.

Linda asked Shannon to bring in pictures of herself as a kid from various ages. If there were pictures of her with her dad, those could be most helpful. They examined the pictures to discover the moment when Shannon's spirited confidence left her face. By age seven it was painfully clear. One picture in particular was of her family taken out-of-doors. Her father had his arm around Shannon, but she was leaning in the opposite direction. The expression on her face was devoid of any confidence and dripping with doubt, so contrary to her carefree expressions in the younger images.

Living with Shannon was difficult, not because of her per se, but because of the circumstances in her life at that moment. It made sense to me then to stick by her in this hard part of her life, that my own feelings and needs seemed understandably secondary. In hindsight I see that this had become a pattern for me, to stick by someone even if it meant giving up large parts of myself. We both saw counselors. Shannon continued to see Linda for individual sessions and she tried a group a few times. Her emotional needs were so high that mine were dwarfed. Any small effort to interest her in life and living was made. When we watched TV, we watched her shows. The songs we listened to were her favorites. When we went to a restaurant, we ordered what she wanted. I didn't even know what my likes and interests were anymore, because they didn't matter. And there certainly was no room in our relationship for me to be weak, for me to cry or require hugs or love. Those were all for her, even if I desperately needed them.

When Chris died I was still living with Shannon at Penn State. It was the summer of 1994; I was 23. It was four years after my final parting with Chris. I got a phone call from my mother. "Have you heard about Chris Douglas?"

"What? Is he getting married?"

"Oh no. No. I guess you haven't heard."

My gut knew instantly. There are only two reasons someone would bring up an ex with you: they got married or they died. Simultaneously I cried and yelled, "What!? He died! Oh my..." The lump forming in my throat stole the last bits of sound out of my mouth. I bawled on the phone, not saying a word, and listened to my mom tell me the story. Shannon sat there just listening and watching.

"He drowned in the Rappahannock River while fishing with his brother and friends. It was on the front page of the local section of the paper."

"Was he married?"

"Yes."

"Does it say to who?"

"Yes, Nadia."

"Yeah, that's who I thought. Did he have kids?"

"No."

"Oh, I guess that's good." *I wonder if she'll be able to move on. I wonder if they were as in love as we were? I wonder if he ever told her about me.* I felt like we had just broken up all over again. This was really final — I wasn't ever going to see him again. Any fantasy I had had about us ever happening again was squashed. I worked myself into a sob at least once a day, but I quickly learned that I couldn't do that at home. Shannon did not understand my grief. Chris was a man after all. Why would a gay woman grieve for a man? I needed her comfort, and she had none for me.

"Shannon, I *loved* him. That is why I'm sad. And I love you. Rest assured, no matter the status of our relationship – whether you are right here living in the same house with me, or whether we have parted ways long ago – when you die, I will be devastated." It's as if I knew that I'd lose her soon as well.

A short time after his death, I crossed paths with Chris's aunt, also a Jehovah's Witness. She said, "Well, you know what we believe happens after death — paradise earth. So maybe there is comfort in that." There wasn't. I resigned to put my chin down and trudge forward with the life I currently had. I learned that through the death of others, many of our own secret hopes and dreams die, too. In hindsight, this could have been the moment that I perked up to notice that death was all about me. But I didn't. I could have noticed that twice now, I had experienced the death of a close peer and could have considered that it might mean something. But I didn't. Not yet. It would take one more.

Shannon and I fought more regularly — most were little spats, but some were big. I thought the fights were good for us, because in the end, they were a form of communication and we got through them fine. But they scared Shannon. Her default thinking was that she was at fault, and that she was causing problems in the relationship. Shannon would blame herself for a whole mess of things that were no one's fault in particular. When we fought, she fled — she'd bolt out the front door and run down the street. I knew she was occasionally suicidal, so I would run out into the night and look around the neighborhood for her. Running was her way to make me physically come to her rescue. Eventually, I figured out that that had to stop. It was too stressful for me. I felt responsible for whether she lived. I told her that I wouldn't chase after her anymore. It didn't mean I didn't care, but it meant that she's in charge of whether she decided to die; not me. If that happened, it wouldn't be my fault, and I was okay with that.

More and more, being around me represented the memories and thoughts she didn't want to have. The memories kept flooding in and became increasingly difficult. The nightmares occurred at least twice a night, and she just wanted a break. She avoided me and our home. Some nights she wouldn't come home. I learned much later that she had even been cheating on me. At the time, I couldn't imagine that someone who was considering death, who was trying to run from a sexually abusive past, might be in the mood for sex. She certainly wasn't in the mood with me. I didn't understand it then, but later I would. It wasn't about the sex.

It seemed obvious to me, that the way for Shannon to grab back control of her life would be for her to deal with these torturous memories and her real-life monster head-on, but she wouldn't. She was reluctant because she was certain she couldn't survive the memories if she allowed all of them to come out. Her therapist explained that this is why she had the nightmares. "What you don't deal with during the day will come out at night." This lesson stuck with me.

Chapter 5

Elizabeth

By April, Shannon and I had agreed that a break from our relationship might be a good idea. She was leaving for a summer internship in Phoenix, Arizona. I also tried to land a summer gig there, but it didn't work out. Thank goodness. Sometimes the greatest gift is to *not* get what you want. Instead, I would be going to South Carolina for my summer internship at a university. Shannon left for her long road trip west on Saturday, April 29. On Wednesday, May 3 she met a new group of friends in her new town; and on Friday, May 12, she had already slept with one of them — Crystal. She had been in town less than two weeks. Two days later she had the decency to call me and tell me what had happened.

For the next two months, before my internship began in South Carolina, I fell into a deep depression. I lost 15 pounds and didn't have 15 pounds to lose. Every waking, and sometimes sleeping, moment was spent thinking of Shannon — our past dialogues, what she was doing now, and what our future might hold. Over the course of the summer, I spent a lot of energy thinking about who I needed to become to be who she needed. I became aware that during our relationship I had given up who I was in order to nurture Shannon's needs, and without her I didn't know who I was. Even in my own good company I was lonely. The break-up and distance was just the wake-up call I needed to face my self-sacrificing and codependent tendencies, but that didn't make it any easier. I needed time to wallow.

On the phone, I told Shannon I needed to get over her, and I did that by asking her to not communicate with me at all for the rest of the summer. Shannon agreed to let me contact her when I was ready, which wouldn't be until the end of the summer. I really struggled to stay out of touch with her. I had become accustomed to being her support. And I continued to believe I was the only one to whom she would turn when she was feeling most vulnerable. I feared that by cutting her off, I was letting her down when she might need me the most. As difficult as it was to not communicate directly with her, I managed to do it. In my personal journal I wrote to her every day the entire summer.

It was during that same summer of 1995 in South Carolina that I met Elizabeth. She was six years older than I, a strawberry blonde with blue eyes and cream-pink skin. Her professionalism, competency, and sense of fun impressed me. For a fluffy kind of gal she enjoyed rockin' out to folk music and hard-hitting women singers, like Melissa Etheridge, especially while driving and beating on her steering wheel. She was quite a reader and wore classic preppy clothes — polos, crisp oxfords, and penny loafers. She smelled like honeysuckle. I wanted to be her friend; I wanted to look up to her. She cracked me up, and she was very sweet.

She was just starting to come out and was thrilled to meet me. Elizabeth wanted a buddy to go to women's bookstores and gay bars with. I showed her the classic lesbian coming out movies: *Desert Hearts*, Mariel Hemingway's *Personal Best*, Susan Sarandon and Catherine Deneuve's *The Hunger*, and *Claire of the Moon*. She ate it all up. Elizabeth had a crush on me, and I thought that was cute. I warned her that I was a hot mess — just dumped and hard. She fell in love with me anyway. And I still thought it was cute. I probably entertained the attention more than I should have. I was happy again and eating well, maybe even feeling love again — and that felt great.

Elizabeth was great company for me that summer, but when I left my summer gig and headed back to my usual life in Pennsylvania, my interest waned.

When the summer ended, I contacted Shannon, terrified that I couldn't handle the communication. I knew I still had feelings for her, but I was mad that I did. I wanted to lash out and yell, but I didn't want to give her that much control over me. I wanted so badly to be done with the emotions of the last several months. The conversation was cordial and plain. It was good to hear her voice again. I tried to sense if she still needed me, but I didn't want her to need me. Or did I? After she consulted with her academic adviser, she decided to stay in Arizona, so she wouldn't be returning to Penn State for the fall term. She'd take her last semester of classes in Arizona and extend her internship at the juvenile delinquency center.

I strung Elizabeth on for nearly four months of a long-distance relationship until it finally all exploded. I told her I wanted to see other people. I wouldn't be able to be faithful. I wanted to be a good person, so I knew I had to tell her. I didn't want to hurt her but I was afraid to lose her friendship. She was the first emotionally healthy, smart, and interesting woman-lover who I'd met yet. But I just wasn't into her enough to forgo just-for-fun others and commit to her.

After I had been wishy-washy and stringing her on for far too long, she finally gave up on me.

"I can't do this anymore," she said. "I can't be your friend who you talk to about your life, and then not be the gal who gets to be with you exclusively. I've gotta stop doing that to myself. It hurts me too much."

Sunday, December 3, 1995 Journal Entry
Last Monday, Elizabeth and I broke up. I just needed to heal from Shannon. I've thought about sucking up everything and going back to her. It's been a rough week. On Friday, I got a birthday card from Shannon. I was angry at it; I hugged it. Today, Elizabeth called to tell me that she didn't want to communicate with me anymore; it's too painful for her. In the middle of our talk, someone called and clicked in. I answered it. It was Shannon's mother, Janice, calling to tell me that Shannon had been killed this morning. I clicked back over to Elizabeth and just bawled and screamed. I hung up with Elizabeth to talk to Janice more. Shannon had been hit by a van. She died on

impact from a traumatic head injury. Service details
would be coming soon.

I called Elizabeth back. She's on her way now.

I called Shannon's girlfriend, Crystal, next. She
said three kids at the juvenile delinquency center had
run away. Center policy required that if any kids were
escaping, the staff had to go after them. Shannon
followed them for a while in her car. Then she chased
them by foot. The kids tried to beat her and kick her
away from them. Shannon got a firm grip on one of the
kids' wrist. His buddies had already made it to the
median of an interstate highway within site of an exit
ramp and bridge. A police officer who had been called to
the scene had parked his car on the bridge to judge where
he should go to help. He saw the whole thing. The older
boys in the median encouraged their buddy to break
free and bolt for the median with them. He did, and
Shannon was quick on his heels without a second beat.
He darted in front of a van and cleared it. Shannon
was hit square-on at full interstate speed. The kids were
charged with homicide. Janice will probably sue the
center for liability for their policy. But Shannon
probably would have run after them anyway.

I remember the phone call with Elizabeth.

"I'm coming up now." Elizabeth was certain.

"Wait, you *just* said you don't want to talk to me
anymore. Remember?"

"Um, Kelly, things just changed."

"But Elizabeth, you can't ask me to think about how I feel
about you. You can't come here and expect me to want to spend
any effort talking, or even thinking, about us."

"I get it. I just want to be there for you."

"Okay, fine."

When she arrived eleven hours later at 5 a.m., she had a
plan.

"Here's the deal. This is what I can agree to. I understand 'us' doesn't matter right now, but I also don't want to let this limbo go on endlessly. I think it's reasonable to say that we don't have to talk about us at all until January. Does that seem fair?"

"I guess it's fair. I don't know how long I'll need though. What if I still don't have room in my brain to think about how I feel about you?"

"Well, we'll talk about it again then. Hopefully, if you aren't in a place to talk about us, you can give me a better idea of when. But, if you can't, or the timing is being drawn out again, then we're no different from where we were yesterday, and I'll have to end this relationship again."

"That sounds fair. How long are you prepared to stay?" I had concert tickets with someone else for that evening, but I didn't mind canceling on her. I preferred to have Elizabeth there to keep me constant company now that death was overwhelming me.

"I can stay for a whole week," which ended up being ideal, because that meant I'd have constant company through the week, through Shannon's memorial service, and a couple days after.

With our deal, I was free to think about Shannon all the time. And I did. All over again. I resented how much of my mental energy Shannon continued to take from me.

I couldn't decide if I was also resentful of spending my entire twenty-fourth birthday at Shannon's memorial. *No birthday celebrations for me this year, today is all about Shannon. Again.*

Shannon's memorial was in her hometown, a three-hour drive away from where I lived. Elizabeth drove me there and served as my moral support. As a favorite of Shannon's mother, I had been invited to the family-only viewing early on the morning of the memorial. Other friends would make the trek out to the memorial, but only a few of us were invited to the morning viewing.

The viewing was in the basement of the funeral home. I was warned that it wasn't intended as a public service. Nothing fancy. No special room, no program, no set-up. This was just our chance to see her body one last time before it was cremated. The basement room looked like a storage room for funeral home supplies — shelves of various altar decor, embalming equipment perhaps, cement floors, basement windows that hugged the ceiling. Shannon was laid out on a steel gurney, covered halfway with a plain white twin bed sheet. Through the sheet, I could see that her left leg had been severely broken, and not reset. She was dressed in a snap-front night gown, grandma-style, with a 1970s bright yellow, pink, and orange floral print. Just a little cheap something to cover her body. She had week-old bedhead that was merely combed through, and caked on beige make-up on all exposed skin to mask her injuries and to disguise her paleness. Her eyes were sunken and sewn shut, having clearly been donated. Her mouth had been visibly sewn shut in an effort to not creep us out if it were inclined to gape open. Her right arm appeared dislocated at her shoulder and was tucked under the sheet. Her left arm and hand were laid out on top of her sheet. I wanted to touch her. I tried to get up the nerve to touch her through the sheet, maybe on the outer edge of her thigh. She looked as though she might feel like a mannequin, hard and hollow. Her beloved Aunt Judy, who had always been on her side, grabbed her hand and lifted it to her own face as she kissed and cried on it. I knew I couldn't do that. I felt like, for once, Shannon needed to be in control of her own body. I changed my mind. I didn't want to touch her.

That body before us was her, alright. I recognized her fingers, her ears, her temple hair. Shannon was lying there dead, and just a few months earlier I was afraid that this would happen, just not quite in this way. Death is what she wanted. She fought hard to survive, sometimes harder than others, but she was attracted to the peace of death. And there it was. I wondered if the accident was a suicide of sorts. Her instincts to jump out of the way, to fight for survival were deadened. Perhaps she saw the van coming, looked right at it, and succumbed to it. Maybe she craved the peace that death offered.

It was good to see her. I missed her, but this was final, clearly over. I wouldn't be having dreams about *her* coming back for me. Seeing her brought the closure for me that I needed. The set-up was crude and possibly alarming for some, but it was perfect for me. She was really dead. I needed to see that. Peace for both of us.

Her cremated remains would be at the memorial service later that evening, so we'd have to figure out how to spend time during the eight hours that it would take to cremate her. Her family invited us over to their house for a small reception.

Shannon's mother greeted me, "Although, I still don't understand it, I know that no man could have loved Shannon with the dedication that you and Crystal did."

"I still love her and always will." My chin quivered, as I tried not to choke up.

"I think Shannon still had feelings for you, too. You just grew apart."

That stuck with me for a while.

"Kelly," she added with a hint of alarm, "I should probably warn you; Shannon's father will be coming to the memorial service this evening."

"Bruce?!"

"Yes. It doesn't make me happy, but he's her father, so...."

Any peace I had been feeling left. At that time, I viewed Bruce with no nuance whatsoever. To me he was pure evil through and through – a criminal daring to walk among us at his victim's funeral.

Elizabeth and I went to a near-by mall with some friends. We shopped and walked. We ended our mall adventure at the food court for dinner before the evening memorial. The scene was surreal — four friends, eating in a mall food court, trying to slow down and take their time, because they were waiting for their friend's body to burn entirely so that they could mourn her. We were all very aware, as we looked around at each other telling Shannon stories, that she was burning at that moment. *Damn. Like something out of a neo-noir, David Lynch movie.*

The memorial brought us back to the funeral home where our day had started. We were on the main floor now, fancy room, decorated with memorabilia. I tried to capture the whole experience in my journal.

41

Friday, December 8, 1995 Journal Entry

The service was nice. I greeted Linda, Shannon's counselor, as she came in. I had invited her. There were picture collages up front. I was in one of them. Ashley, a stuffed elephant that I gave her last Christmas, was there. Also one of the pictures showed her in my old college sweatshirt.

Then Bruce came in. I went to Aunt Judy and bitched with her. She said no one knew better than I what Shannon went through with him. True. Apparently, Judy and Shannon had planned on confronting him together after her graduation in January. Judy still planned on doing it.

After the service, as we filed out toward the lobby, I was directly behind Bruce. My face burned hot and my hands clammed up cold. I delighted in following him with an overwhelming sense of revenge. I wanted to make a scene; I did not want to make a scene. I didn't seem to have control of my arms when I reached toward him. Elizabeth grabbed my hands and stopped me. Bruce kept walking and joined the receiving line. I could not stand to see him in the receiving line, so I darted out of the building onto a porch and rested by the outside wall. My friends followed me and tried to distract me with calm talk about the service. I was filled with a fulminating rage that coursed through me. I wanted to kill Bruce. Then, he walked out of the building and stood directly in front of me on the porch. I was later told that I slammed my body back against the building. With clenched fists I slow-motion punched a friend in the stomach as she moved between Bruce and me.

He stood there fairly oblivious, but I could tell that the people around him knew I was looking right at him with rage. A friend told me to walk, so my group took me to the sidewalk. I saw Linda and called for her.

I hugged her and shook as if I were cold. She knew. She said, "It's Bruce, isn't it?" I nodded. I trembled and shook not knowing why because it wasn't very cold out. Then Elizabeth hurried to get the car for me. A friend hugged me, and I collapsed from exhaustion. My body had been tense, then I fell fast. I really believed I would have killed that man. My body was limp and every muscle sore. Elizabeth pulled the car around, scooped me in, and took me home.

I would later come to understand that what I had experienced was shock. The intensity of fierce, yet restrained emotions, the tightness, the shaking, and the sudden utter exhaustion — that was shock.

In the car ride back home, I reflected. *I wanted to kill him? Really?*

I decided that I probably didn't, though I had fantasies about it. I didn't want to be connected to Bruce forever in any way, even in revenge. I wasn't even sure that I wanted him to die. What I wanted was justice, and I knew his death wouldn't bring that. I wanted him to be accountable for what he did; I wanted him in prison. I was deeply troubled that no one kept Bruce out of the event, that no one called him out, that he was allowed to be in that space that was supposed to be dedicated to honoring Shannon's life. I wondered if the person who should have kept him out, who should have called him out, was me. Perhaps that's what had fueled my ire. *What responsibility do I have now?* I fantasized about sending him letters addressed from Shannon with haunting messages of abuse memories that she had told me about. That I'd mail them any time I went to a new city to keep him nervous. But I didn't want to connect myself to him in any way. I wanted to move on. I knew how to do that, to walk away from people I have intense feelings for. This time it wasn't love though; this was hate.

As years went by, I've looked back at Bruce and understood him to be an extreme example of "hurt people hurt people." *What in the world had happened to him?* Not as an excuse for what he had done to Shannon, but an explanation.

Shannon had too long understood his actions as what she had deserved, which I never believed, but over time I began to see it as an expression of his own pain. It wasn't really about her. "You are not what has been done to you," I wish I could tell her now. But that's a lesson I need for myself, too.

At the memorial, the significance of my life circumstances had not yet caught my attention. Sure, I knew that this was my third peer death, my second ex, and that it was also my birthday – but that any of that would mean anything was still beyond me. If the universe wanted me to pay attention, I'd need a more obvious message. In a matter of days, the messages would become clearer.

In the days and weeks that followed the service, Elizabeth's sense of compassion and attentiveness impressed me. It had to be hard for her to see me so worked up about another woman. Shannon surely didn't appreciate seeing me mourn Chris, but Elizabeth didn't feel that way at all. She supported me, hugged me, asked good questions, and listened to me ramble on and on about Shannon. She was happy to have me literally cry on her shoulder at my ex's memorial service. Elizabeth was the first relationship I had been in where someone made a sacrifice for *me*. She took a week off from work to support me in this awkward time. I didn't know that there was a test for her to pass, but this was it.

Chapter 6

The Prophets Jeff and Nancy

I continued to have a hard time dealing with the grief. When Shannon died, it was my finals week in graduate school, and I had no interest in studying, writing, reading, or even being a student. I only wanted to think back on every memory that I had with Shannon, trying to remember everything. I wrote quite a bit. I gathered together any of her friends I could think of and we'd sit around crying, laughing, and telling Shannon stories. I deferred my finals; I wasn't sure if I'd ever want to take them.

With Shannon's death, I wasn't sure how to get through my final exams. I was too stunned to think about how I would get through the days let alone tests. I just woke up each morning, and it was a curious feeling.

Oh, I woke up. Why am I here? Oh, because I am alive? But why?

I'd put my feet on the floor and go through my day. I didn't have a plan for how to manage, but in effect I just lived each day as it came. And my finals, well, I couldn't study. I knew I had to tell my professors what was happening.

Since Elizabeth was in town, she offered to come to classes with me just to sit there. If I broke down, she'd be there. I wouldn't be alone as I walked through my days. Before my counseling theory class, Elizabeth took a seat next to where I usually sat. I wanted to tell the professor that I had a guest and I wanted him to know why. We stood near the doorway of the class as classmates filed in past us.

"Jeff, hi, I wanted to let you know something. Um," I paused. *How am I going to say this?*

The professor turned his eyes to me, "Yes?"

"Um, well, I brought a guest today, and I hope that's okay."

"Oh sure," and he started to pivot away.

"Well, there's more. Um, I wanted to tell you why."

"Oh, it's okay, I'm open to guests. I don't need to know why."

"But I *want* you to know."

And he turned to look at me more attentively.

"I, um. My ex died this weekend. And I'm struggling a bit to get through without crying, so I have a friend here in case I lose it."

"Oh wow," and he stepped a bit closer, and I caught the intensity of his blue eyes. "I'm so sorry."

"I don't know what to do about the final. I hope you'll consider an incomplete. I don't think I can do a final now, and I'm really not sure when."

"Oh, no, don't worry about it." He looked at the ceiling. "I mean at all. I'll look at your current grade in the class, and let you know what it is. And you can have that, without the final, if you want it. Your choice."

My head nodded backwards as if his news had hit me in the face. "Whoa, really? That would be great. I know what my grade is, so, yeah, I'll take it. I really appreciate that. It's a relief, actually." I felt my chest take a breath, and I shifted to walk to my seat.

"So wait, I should tell you." He hesitated. "I, um, I had a dream about you this week."

What? Me?! There are 40 people in this class. How do you even know my name, let alone have dreams about me?

"And I wasn't going to tell you because it seemed inappropriate and too creepy that your professor had a dream about you. But now, with this," he gestured toward my heart. "I feel like I need to tell you."

I was floored, it *did* seem creepy. But I was curious, "What was it about?"

"Actually, it was vague. But I woke up with a strong sense that you were in trouble and needed help."

I let out a quick laugh, "Oh, funny. Almost true, but I wasn't the one in trouble."

"Oh, but I think you are."

Am I? Are you right? But I feel okay. My face wrinkled with confusion. "Oh, I'm okay. She was just an ex. I'll be okay. Just a little stunned for now."

"Well, I want you to know that I'm thinking of you, and if you need support through this, I can do that."

"Thanks for the offer. I am surrounded by friends right now," and I looked at Elizabeth who was looking back at me. "I'll be okay." And I returned to my desk for class.

At the time I appreciated Jeff's message as an acknowledgment that this loss was indeed hard. Over twenty years later I had nearly forgotten about this conversation until I serendipitously met one of Jeff's recent advisees. The memories came back as I told my story to my new friend who agreed that Jeff is deep like that. Suddenly with hindsight, I understood that larger forces were at work to tell me to "pay attention" to the hardness because I would have a longer journey of loss ahead of me.

Later that week, I met with my master's adviser during her office hours. I poked my head in the door to see if she was there. Her back was to the door as she faced her desk computer.

"Hi, Nancy?" I tried to get her attention.

"Oh, hi Kelly. Come on in."

"Do you have a moment?"

"Um, well, if you need a long moment, I should drop off this form to my secretary first. She's been waiting on it."

"I'm not sure how long this will take."

"Well, let me go ahead and do this, and I'll be back."

She twisted her swivel chair around toward me and used both of her hands to scoop each of her braced legs out from under her. She locked each knee joint into place. She reached for her crutches, and she was off. "I'll just be a moment." But the deepest impact of our meeting would come before she even returned. I sat in a chair next to her tall filing cabinet and faced her desk with my back to the door. I looked around at her book titles and pictures of her with famous authors in our field. Of course *she* was a famous author in our field, too. On the filing cabinet right next to my head was a large magnet that read, "The Rules for Being Human," with a list of ten rules.[1] I started reading them, and rule two jumped out at me, "You will be presented with lessons. These lessons are specific to you, and learning them is the key to discovering and fulfilling the meaning and relevance of your own life."

Oh, that's...that's for me. That message is for me right here, right now. This hardness? This struggle to get through this day? This is for me. I'm going to learn something from this. This made sense to me. *Okay, what's next.*

I scanned ahead and rule four caught my eye, "The lesson is repeated until learned. ... Lessons will repeat until you see them as such and learn from them. ... Also fundamental is the acceptance that you are not a victim of fate or circumstance ...things happen to you because of how you are and what you do."

I did this? Was there a lesson in losing Chris that I didn't get? Is this my fault? What am I supposed to learn from this? The part of me that interpreted the deaths as having "happened to me" felt that this magnet was telling me that my loved ones were dying *because* of me and "how I am and what I do." Somehow that felt true to me, that there had been lessons available to learn from my college suite-mate's death and from Chris's death, but I hadn't learned them yet – that "how I am" is a person who has been impervious to the lessons. And so the lesson presented itself again. Why *wouldn't* I think that?! How unusual to experience three unrelated peer deaths by the age of 24? Why wouldn't I think that it had to mean something specific to me...especially with this magnet sitting there telling me that it was so. Of course, there was another part of me, the skeptic, that said all of that was poppycock. But still I held the message, that there were lessons for me in these death experiences.

Now, reflecting back on this moment with the magnet, I see that I yearned for a spiritual explanation for this unlikely series of events, but I had cut off that part of me. At that point of

---

[1] The magnet was from "The Rules for Being Human" attributed to "Anonymous" in the *Chicken Soup for the Soul* in 1993. In 1998 the author, Cherie Carter-Scott, stepped forward and published her rule in a book, *If Life is a Game, These are the Rules*.

my life, and for many years to come, I wouldn't be looking to religion to explain any of my losses, and I hadn't developed an explicit spiritual life to replace it. Instead, at that moment, I was open to receiving messages from a magnet.

There, I suppose, is where the true lesson really lay, had I had the maturity and life experience to connect the dots. If my now-self could have talked to my then-self, I would have said, "Deaths are not the lessons in and of themselves. Death just happens; indeed it's a part of life. Deaths will continue to happen if you learn lessons or not. What will keep happening, though, until you learn the lesson, is the quality of how you grieve. Until you find meaning in death you will continue to fear it. To find meaning in death, and indeed in life, is to find a spiritual path. *That's* your quest."

Instead, I had assumed that if the repeated deaths were about me, then I was responsible for them continuing to happen. I thought, if I could change me, I could control life events. *I have to learn this lesson. I have to. What am I resisting? What lesson do I need? Why can't I see the lesson?*

In the short time that I waited for Nancy, my view of life had shifted. I connected Jeff's message to me via his dream and these 'rules' from Nancy's magnet. I could see a calling to pay attention and to seek learning – and thus began the very beginnings of my quest for a spiritual life. Messages were getting through.

All of this is about me. Something did just happen to me, not just to someone else, and it has happened before. And it will happen again, if I don't learn the lessons that I'm supposed to learn.

The fact that time, and the lives of others, dared to go on was audacious to me. I was shocked to discover that time doesn't stop to memorialize those we've lost. It has no idea. My overwhelming consumption with thoughts about death also included being faced with my own mortality. I could die at any moment. I questioned how I chose to spend my time. If I die next week, do I really want to have spent my last days writing a difficult paper? Probably not. Long-term investments of time did not seem like time well spent. I kept telling myself that I would most likely live long enough for my graduate studies to be a worthy investment of my time, but I was faced with clear evidence that there were no guarantees. It took me another six months before I could commit again to my graduate program.

Shannon did graduate from Penn State, posthumously. She had completed enough of her fall credits to pass the courses. I took and passed my remaining finals in January, and struggled academically through the next term.

Elizabeth and I met up again in mid-January to talk through our relationship, and I was mostly set. I told her that I wanted her to love Shannon. She said she would as long as she felt secure with me. She said it was painfully obvious how in love I still was at the services. After meeting up for one weekend in Roanoke, Virginia, we decided to commit to each other for the long haul. And we stayed together another eight years, through Elizabeth's move to Pennsylvania, a move to Chicago together, several job changes for each of us, the purchase of a house, the beginning of my doctoral studies, the adoption of two dogs, and two unsuccessful inseminations. In addition, more lessons from being close to death were coming whether I was going to learn from them or not.

Chapter 7

Nick

Nick was my boss in Chicago where we worked at Northwestern University together. I first met him in 1998 when he hired me; I was 26. My office was right next door to his. Our supervisory meetings were mostly about personal life updates. Since he'd grown up in the area, his community connections were deep. "Ya know, what you need to try? That Pancake House up in Wilmette. Amazing." "There's a fantastic, hidden, up-scale restaurant right around the corner from the train station – you have to check that out." "The most personable family doctor in town is Dr. Tuccillo, you should to go see her." "Yeah, next time you need a mechanic, you have to go to Dave on Dempster." Nick was Mr. Community. Nick was Mr. Resource. When I needed help with taxes, he knew who I should see. When we talked about life philosophies, I was all talk. He recommended a book called *The Celestine Prophecy*. He brought it up a few times, but I never read it. I wasn't *that* into life philosophies. I shared stories of learning from life events and paying attention to a certain degree, but I wasn't interested in overarching philosophies yet. There's a saying that some attribute to the Buddha, "When the student is ready, the teacher will appear." I can look back on my life and at multiple points see that the teacher was there, but the student wasn't ready.

Nick was also Mr. Family. His boys were middle-school aged. They would come hang out at the office sometimes when they were out of school. His wife was a vice president at a nearby community college. They had been high school sweethearts who met in middle school at a summer camp and were still so connected to each other's hopes, dreams, and lives.

Nick was not Mr. Outgoing; more like Mr. Reserved. He'd much rather talk with you one on one in his office than give a speech to a big group, though he could hold his own on a stage. He was shorter than the average American man, about my height, tan, with a head of thick wavy brown hair.

Nick's favorite time of year was graduation. He enjoyed seeing the students at their best, especially since, as a dean, he had seen many of them over the years at their worst. Each year he made a point to attend, and sometimes even helped officiate the baccalaureate service. He enjoyed the smaller venue and the more intimate crowd than the larger graduation ceremony. One year I caught him smiling and almost giggling through one of the hymns. I thought he must be having a good time.

"That looked like fun for you."

"That hymn always cracks me up. It's the only time of year I get to hear that hymn, and it just floors me."

"Which hymn?"

"Didn't you hear the words? 'Classrooms and labs!? Loud boiling test tubes!? Sing to the Lord a new song! Athlete and band, loud cheering people, Sing to the Lord a new song!' [2] I just picture the bubbling test tubes, and I crack up. It's a hymn and it has the words 'test tube' in it! There's nothing better than that." Nick would later request this hymn for his memorial service.

I had worked with Nick for four years before his health started playing tricks on him. Chris and Shannon died suddenly in tragic accidents, but Nick was dying slowly before my eyes. It's hard to say what exactly was killing Nick. Cancer is the easy answer, but which kind? Something unique enough that doctors never knew quite what it was — some sort of cross between a bone/skin/lymph-node cancer.

Symptoms started with a numb pinky finger that he could move one day but not the next. Then it would be two fingers. Then movement would come back again. Then he had similar challenges with his feet. One foot would drag as he walked, then

---

[2] "Earth and All Stars" lyrics by Herbert F. Brokering, tune by David N. Johnson, 1964 for the 90th anniversary of St. Olaf College. Source: Hymnary.com retrieved January 15, 2015.

it wouldn't. He tripped quite a bit and laughed it off with his good nature. Doctors did tests, and equipped him with finger and foot splints, but it seemed to get progressively more concerning. Finally one day they decided to do a cancer screening. With the definitive results, suddenly his symptoms made sense; then they didn't again. Bone cancer cells showed up in his skin, but there were none in his bones. Cancer moved around his lymph-nodes. Docs were baffled and came up with creative treatment plans.

At the same time that Nick was living and working with cancer, so was another co-worker, Miriam. Miriam was an acquaintance to me, a close friend of a close friend of mine, so we ended up in common social circles together – we celebrated New Year's Y2K together – but never talked beyond superficial pleasantries. I mean, she had cancer and I didn't feel close enough to her to talk about those types of things.

I also had a hard time knowing what to say to Nick when I saw him at work. I could try to talk about the weather, or a work situation. I had no idea what to say to a man who was faced head-on with his life. Sometimes I would get brave, and I'd ask how he was feeling. If it was good news I was set. If it was bad news, I had nothing. *How do I respond? No idea.* He could see right through me. He was great. He'd know just what to say to take the pressure off of me to say just the right encouraging thing.

Once he told a fascinating story about being asked to attend an oncology conference as an unusual case. The MDs were supposed to read his chart, then walk in the room, ask him questions, and share their opinions. He agreed to do it thinking that someone out there might have a helpful perspective, but as soon as it began, he regretted it. He sat in nothing but a hospital gown as well dressed (mostly) men in white coats talked about him and around him, and directly in front of him. Few read the chart and instead asked him to repeatedly tell his own medical history over and over. There was no regard from the docs that it might be difficult to tell strangers that you are dying. *Read the damn chart.* It was humiliating for him. *Yeah, damn doctors. Great story, Nick. Thanks for that.* Nick always had an interesting and engaging story to tell, and that's what I counted on to maintain our relationship. I had nothing.

Others at work seemed to know how to connect with him. I was clueless; but they knew. They'd chat with him about regular life stuff, cancer would come up, and they'd make some sensitive heart-felt comment. There'd be a genuine tear, maybe a hug, and the conversation would wrap up with an appropriate joke and a smile. *That was classy. That was good. I could try that.* But I couldn't. I didn't know how to make small talk with someone with cancer. I knew when speaking to someone with cancer that their feelings should be center stage; but I also knew I had some serious baggage related to death. I worried that too many of my own feelings would come up, and I didn't trust that I could get through an interaction with Nick without completely blowing it.

As Nick went through chemo, he continued to work with us, even through his discomfort. He took other medications to ease the symptoms from the chemo. He became more goofy and outgoing than usual, making corny jokes that just weren't his style. He had never been Mr. Cheese, but now he was. We wondered if it was some type of psychological coping mechanism — maybe he was trying to find humor in life in a forced and desperate way. Nick eventually explained to us that his personality was changing due to a side effect from one of his medications. He didn't like it. He didn't feel comfortable in his body, but it gave him energy that he needed to get through the day.

One day he gave a welcoming address to an auditorium of about 200 students. We staff members sat in the front row of the audience. He welcomed the group with a look in his eyes that wasn't his own. He lost his way through his words; he cracked stupid jokes. It was kind of sweet at first, until it occurred to me why this was happening. That wasn't him up there, but the students didn't know that. We did. A colleague next to me, one who was always friendly with me, looked at me with the most perplexed and worried face that she could muster, and I nodded in agreement. We both started to tear up at the same time. Sniff. Wipe. The whole front row was holding back sobs as Nick gave his clown talk. When it was over, we talked with him – or rather my well-spoken colleague did – and he knew what had happened, but he was at a loss. "I just don't know what else to do. This is probably the new me for a while." These students weren't going to get to know that Nick is a really cool guy for them to have in their lives.

When Nick's health got so poor that he went into the hospital, I was terrified to visit him. My coworkers would go together in groups; I kept putting it off. *What would I say to him? Would it be fair to depend on him to carry the conversation and keep me comfortable? What if I freaked out and cried? That wouldn't be helpful at all. It would be selfish of me to cry in front of him.* I felt that that's just the sort of thing I thought I would do, and it would be so wrong. I preferred not to go at all, for his sake. That was fall 2003.

A few months later in November, I met an incredible man named Dan at a conference. Dan recommended a book to me, *The Celestine Prophecy.* We instantly connected and I knew that meeting Dan was a life-changing moment, so reading that book seemed especially important since it also represented a connection to Nick. The book is a fable that lays out a holistic philosophy of life. The first principle is that there is no such thing as coincidence. It was no coincidence that a new yet familiar person came into my life and told me to read this book that would lay out some beautiful beliefs, some of which Nick held. I thought this book could be my "in" with Nick. I returned home, checked out the book from the library, and quickly read it.

Just when I was convincing myself to go visit Nick, to find a date on my schedule when I would most definitely go see him, he died. I was too late. He died on my 32nd birthday — *Yes, Universe, I'm paying attention.*

Among my work colleagues, we all feared that Nick would die, but when he did, we just weren't prepared. We didn't allow ourselves to talk about or even believe he was dying. But he was dying.

I didn't get to visit him to say goodbye. Or hello. I think I wrote a message in a book of reflections that had been made for him, but I didn't tell him to his face. He was special, and I didn't get to tell him that I felt that way.

I felt horrible.

Nick had two memorial services: one at the chapel at our work place for his professional family, and another at a camp out in the far western Chicago suburbs for family, close friends, and long-lost friends. Work colleagues close enough to Nick knew that the line between his work life and home life was thin. For the most part, Nick lived a whole life, not segmented. Many of us in his department went to both services. We felt like family. And since I didn't manage to go visit him in the hospital, I felt especially compelled to attend everything I could now. Maybe somehow he could at least see that. *I do care; I just suck at showing it.* While attending these memorial services with a colleague, I found someone who could help me on my journey to find a more open and honest way to deal with death.

Chapter 8

Miriam

Just weeks before Nick's death, I had heard that Miriam's three-year-long remission was over. The cancer was back. I worked closely enough with her that I saw her regularly and heard vague rumors about her health updates. Personal health and the prospect of death seemed private enough to me that I never asked her about it. I didn't want to be nosy; it was none of my business. And, although I was curious to learn more about her and I felt experienced with losing people to death by now, I was also uncomfortable about being close to death. I had avoided the topic with Miriam too, and she humored me. Through small talk with her I pretended life was trudging along normally for both of us. Honestly, I didn't even know if Miriam knew that I knew about her cancer. *Was I even supposed to know?* So, I ignored it. Miriam was pretty easy to talk to every time I had the chance to speak with her; if it wasn't for the fact that she was, you know, maybe dying, I might have been more interested in being her friend.

Sometime soon after Nick's death, my work tasks brought me to Miriam's office for a consult. Thankfully, she brought up what was on both of our minds.

"Terrible news about Nick, Kelly."

"Yes. Yes it is," I replied. Unsaid: *Terrible news about you, too, Miriam.*

"How is your team holding up?"

Us? How about you? Miriam, how can you not be thinking of your own mortality right now? Is this conversation really about Nick? "Well, we're obviously sad. Devastated, actually. As for our day-to-day impact, we managed to accommodate his absence long ago, so fortunately we're all just grieving, and not also having to figure out how to do our jobs without him." *And, Miriam, I'm sure if you died we would be devastated, too.*

"Are you going to the chapel service?"

"Absolutely!" *Are you? I mean would you even want to? Wouldn't that be some form of torture? Miriam, you really seem like a very interesting person whom I would like to know more. Um, so, would you let me be your friend? You see, I have to process with someone what I did to Nick, by ignoring him in his final days. Can that be you? You have an informed perspective. Will you allow me to feel close to you so that I can feel better about myself? Through you, can I make up for Nick? Through you, can I grow into the decent human being I hope that I am? Will you be my friend?* "So, do you want to go with me?"

"That's a great idea."

Miriam and I went to the chapel memorial together. We sang the boiling test tube hymn, with smirks on our faces in remembrance of Nick. But when the eulogies began, the mood turned somber. I felt more comfortable with death than with the dying. I can be sad, deeply sad; I'm comfortable with that. I welcome it when times are sad; the deep sadness is a release. I just fear being *that* sad in front of a dying person; it feels selfish. *I can't let myself be sad in front of people who are affected more immediately than I am.*

The chapel memorial service presented an awkward opportunity. I could be visibly sad, and I could cry and sob. And I could do it right in front of a dying person — because it wasn't about her. Or at least, I could mask it that way.

During the entire service I mourned for Nick, but I thought of Miriam. She made no hint that she might have been thinking of herself during the service. Afterwards, Miriam and I walked out together; she made some comment about the cruelty of cancer, and I thought, *This is my chance.*

"So I'm curious how you can be here. Like, what is it like to be here? What is running through your mind?"

"Nick is on my mind. This is all about him. This isn't about me."

And I truly believed her. "Sure. Right, but you have a perspective here that I don't have."

"I could bring that here and allow it to cloud all I see, but it's harder to experience life when it's filtered in that way. Right now, I am all about experiencing life as best as I can. My focus is on Nick."

"You are amazing, Miriam. What you say makes perfect sense. I'm in awe, because I think I'm too self-absorbed to be able to do that."

"Kelly, I really like you. Most people don't want to talk to me about these kinds of thoughts. But this has given me a chance at some clear thinking on life, and I'd love to talk more about it." Pause. "Just," her eyes shifted, "right now is not the time."

"Right. Yes. Hey, I'd love to get together and really talk."

"Definitely, and I want to hear more about your life, your doctoral studies, and how your relationships are going. I hear you have news about meeting someone."

Smiling, "Yes, We'll do that." I hoped this was genuine on her part. It was on mine. Too often people say "let's get together" out of some polite obligation, all the while knowing that they won't — either they aren't really that interested, or they are but have little time to work it into a busy life.

A few days later, Miriam and I traveled together to Nick's memorial service that was intended for family and community. Other colleagues came separately. I've never had a connection to a place like Nick and Elaine had. They met at a summer camp as middle-schoolers. They came back every summer to reunite. As older high schoolers, then college students, they were camp counselors together. They got married at the camp. It made sense to have his memorial at the camp lodge. Nick had requested it. It was packed. The lodge wasn't built to accommodate the masses of friends and family who would mourn an active middle-aged caring community man. Packed. Rows and rows of folding chairs, people sitting in aisles, leaning against the log cabin walls. Everywhere people were squeezed in. Tribute after tribute. The program was long. Many people wanted to speak about Nick. His brother looked and sounded so much like him. His friends and colleagues throughout the years shared stories — stories about

Nick growing up on the property, stories of him taking a swim in the lake on his wedding day. The final speaker listed in the program was his wife. His wife. She was going to speak, and I just couldn't imagine her being able to speak. She was wonderful. Her voice was clear. She was real. She led us all through the toughest parts of her grief like a competent tour-guide. She made three points that I will never forget and often retell.

First, she told of his last days, and how he was being forced to leave his beloved wife and sons. They obviously didn't want him to go, but he didn't want to go, either. It was like a forced break-up. "I want nothing more than to love you every day, but I can't." His experience reminded me of my awful break-up with Chris. Two people madly in love, breaking up anyway. How powerless that feels. She expected there to be a time when he'd be more resigned to dying, and it seemed it would never come. He did not want to part this life no matter how lethargic or painful he felt. She loved that about him. She'd hold him in his hospital bed, lie down, and cozy right up next to him, and try to hold him into this life, to keep him from slipping away. When the time finally did come, he said, "I think I'm ready," but he also added, "and it's going to be okay." And he died just an instant later. He held on loving and fighting for love as long as he could.

Second, she asked us if we felt there was anyone in the world who truly "gets you." Someone who celebrates your great days. Who forgives your bad ones, because they get the real you and understand why the bad stuff sometimes happens. They get the bigger context of you. Someone who knows just what you need before you know for yourself. I wondered if anyone in my life ever had. Certainly not Chris, Maria, or Shannon – and probably not even Elizabeth. I'd felt misunderstood. I'd felt under appreciated. We get wrapped up in our own selves. We forget that others have struggles. Honestly, I don't think I'd even known someone in that way. I hoped that I could find that mutual connection someday, maybe someday soon. Elaine explained that Nick truly knew her. "And now, he's gone." With that comment I felt her emptiness with her. She told one story of an evening when she came home late from work frazzled about the day's stressful events. She had not called ahead to warn Nick that he'd be on his own with the boys that night; there had been no time for that with the day she had. Elaine came through the door wondering if she had worried Nick, but he handed her a glass of wine. He wanted to hear about her day. He had drawn a hot bubble bath for her. Rather than being upset with her for missing dinner and bedtime with the boys without notice, he had taken care of everything — the dinner, the boys, and her. She asked us, "Can you imagine? How lucky was I? And this was just one example. He often thought of me and what I needed before I even knew. What a guy! We should all be loved like that." Her use and comfort with the word *was* struck me in the throat.

Third, Elaine explained that their experience with Nick's cancer afforded them the opportunity to learn who their true friends were. In this time of amazing despair, people had retouched their lives, in new and deeper ways. Elaine and Nick had felt blessed to have such deep friendships. Elaine explained that death brings clarity to life. The meals, the pumpkin bread, phone calls from past fond folks, visitors — they were profound gestures that exposed to them who their true friends were. I knew I wasn't one. I didn't pass the test.

In the weeks that followed, Miriam and I developed a regular routine. We'd get together for dinners or drinks to tell our stories. We tried to hit weekly, but the frequency was mostly dictated by her chemo schedule. Right afterwards she was too tired. Right before there was too much discomfort and pain.

Miriam and I were a good match. We were both introverts and didn't want to be bothered with small talk. I can still hear her voice: calming, wise clarity of insight with every word. We cut straight to the deep stuff.

I asked her what life was like for her now. I wanted to ask if she was dying, but I felt that was the most insensitive question I could possibly ask. Besides, I knew she didn't truly know. I asked for medical updates. She'd already had a double mastectomy about three years earlier, the first time she'd kicked cancer's butt. But now that the breast cancer was back, it was obviously no longer in her breasts. It was in her lower back, near her pelvis. It was sore to sit sometimes. I learned chemo is not just one drug. Apparently there are several drugs that can be tried. If cancer doesn't respond to one, doctors can reevaluate and try another. Miriam had tried nearly all of them, but tumors continued to multiply up her spine. So far, and fortunately, they were staying away from her organs. She had only one more option left if the current drug she was on didn't work.

She told stories of how differently people related to her now. I was one case in point, for sure. She joked, "Oh, now you want to know me?!" Miriam explained that the cancer and the possibility of dying provided her so much clarity in life. "You really learn who your real friends are."

"Oh Miriam, I hurt when I hear that. I've heard that before." Tears welled in my eyes. "I'm afraid Nick may have said something similar about me...I...I couldn't be around him. I didn't know how to make conversation with him anymore. I faded away. And I'm sure he interpreted that to mean I wasn't a real friend."

"Kelly, that's not what I'm talking about. I get, and I'm sure Nick got, that people mourn differently. And the mourning starts while you are still living. Some people want to talk and cry with you, even if you don't want to cry. Some bring you food and no talk, only sympathetic smiles and off-topic conversations. And, yes, some do fade away. But they all are friends. Grief isn't just happening to me, but to all the people around me. I'm the centerpiece of it. Nick knew that, too. He knew you cared.

"No, what I'm talking about are those relationships that have always been hard work," she continued. "They just aren't worth it." Relationships she would have struggled to navigate in the past, she now realized, are too much effort, so she just let them go.

I told her of my guilt about Nick. Miriam's interpretation made perfect sense, or perhaps I just wanted it to, because in this version of the story I was a fine, but grieving person.

At our next meeting I was excited to tell Miriam about a dream I'd had about Nick. There was so much clarity to the dream that I'd wondered if Nick had visited me in the dream to deliver a very clear and forgiving message. In the dream I walked nervously through the hallway of a hospital. Every patient's room door was closed — a corridor of closed doors. I closely examined every door for the number, until I came to one that I thought might be Nick's. Before I knocked on the door, I thought about what I might say. What could I say that might bring happiness or hope to him, but still honor the gravity of the situation? I didn't know, but I knocked on the door anyway.

Nick opened the door himself. He had on a hospital gown that opened in the back, but was modestly drawn. Bare feet. He looked great — healthy with a glow, like his pre-sick self. "Hey, Kelly, I'm glad you made it. Come on in." There were others in the room seated in chairs near his empty bed. As Nick extended his arm to motion for me to enter the room, I saw behind him and his seated guests that the room extended into the size of a ballroom filled with mingling people. Nick politely welcomed me, but my arrival clearly interrupted a conversation that he was eager to get back to. "There are people here who you know. Go ahead and mingle and enjoy yourself." *Of course the room was packed.*

All of my rehearsing and nervousness was for naught, as Nick didn't depend on me to have some message. He was surrounded by people who loved and cared for him. He didn't need me. He probably never even wondered where I was. Or if he did, he most certainly never fretted over it. How self-involved of me to think that how I mourned would matter to Nick.

Miriam told me of her growing up years being an only child and adopted by Jewish parents. Miriam knew she was of Jewish ethnicity by birth since that's what her adoptive parents were looking for when they found and fell in love with her as a baby. The adoption meant that she had limited-to-no bone marrow matches, so a marrow transplant was not an option.

We swapped love-life stories. She was 46 and single, and had had a few lengthy relationships, all with men named Jack. Three to be exact. I told her of my two dead exes. That was my thing. Her thing was Jacks. One Jack was married; Miriam was the other woman. He was a former professor of hers. They used to swap love letters hand-written in cursive. They'd exchange gifts of stationery, wax sealers, and fancy pens. So romantic! My stories were about my dead exes, and about having just met Dan a few months earlier. My relationship with Dan was long distance, with me in Chicago and him in Virginia. We'd get together every three weeks, and I reported to Miriam how our meet-ups went. While my attraction to Dan was less of a surprise to me, it was a worthy topic of conversation with my friends who had thought of me as gay. I told Miriam of Dan's plans to move to Chicago to be with me and that the gesture felt like the kind of sacrifice that I needed a partner to make for me. Miriam approved.

In the early 2000s my dream car was a gun-metal-grey Jetta sedan, with the blue lit-up dials on the dashboard. Slick. I was quick to spot them in town and would point the car out to anyone nearby. "That's a cool car." I drove a sensible plastic-bodied Saturn sedan in hunter green. I pulled into my work parking lot one day, where I was familiar with all of the cars and their corresponding owners, and I saw one of those slick Jetta bullets. I was thrilled to later learn it was Miriam's new car. *You go, girl!*

At our next dinner out, Miriam explained her buying process. It was her dream car, too. But like me, she'd always been taught to purchase used cars. The Jetta's monthly payment was too expensive on the 60-month plan, and she'd been taught to be wary of using the full 60 months — too much interest paid, too much risk of the car dying sooner than it would be paid for.

But something clicked for Miriam. In that car lot her paradigm for evaluating the worth and risk of things had dramatically shifted. She thought about the 60-month plan and realized that it would likely outlive her. Damn car.

So she asked the salesperson how long the car loan would have to be to get the monthly payments where she could afford the car. Answer 90 months, a 7.5 year loan. Sold! She realized that she only needed to afford the car on a monthly basis, that if the loan would outlive her anyway, why not take advantage of that. The assumptions she had always made about the future were drastically changing. Miriam's new mantra was to enjoy life now. Buy the cool car, do the insensible thing. Go out with more experiences lived.

Miriam already loved her job, her life, her friends, so she didn't make drastic changes. But she sought adventures. She drove that cool car, and she traveled to her dream destinations. She went to China and England. She connected with favorite aunts and cousins. I admired her perspective and decision to not only live in the present but to find genuine value in her situation.

Though I knew the building she lived in, I had never been in her condo. And I didn't know any of our mutual friends who had. She had always been private. Some things seemed off limits. As Miriam's condition deteriorated, she was more difficult to connect with. She just didn't feel up to visiting with anyone. I assumed it was the same treatment issue that she had been having all long. And as I got closer to completing my dissertation writing, my life focus became narrow. I wrote all day, every day, for seven days a week. I even skipped Christmas that year. I didn't push or inquire about Miriam. I let my relationship with her shift to the background for a few months. Without really thinking it through, I'm sure I counted on reconnecting with her once my paper was finished. My final paper was on track to be turned in by early July 2006, but she died in early June. *Damn.* Again, I didn't get to say good-bye. I didn't know the end was so close. What I had thought to be drug-related lethargy was her learning that her last hope of medication was not working. She was off treatment medications and had turned to comfort ones. She told mutual friends to keep the news from me, to let me focus on my writing. I didn't know.

I attended her service, the only Jewish funeral I'd ever attended. It was just as she had described it to me. During one of our dinner conversations, she told me that she designed her service herself. At the ceremony her voice was clear in my head, as I saw each detail that she described to me come to life. As I looked around the synagogue from where I sat, I saw the details of the room that she had described to me, open-fan seating, simple adornment. As her casket was brought into the synagogue and lifted high and carried around the room, I remembered how she lit up when she told me how delighted she was with that Jewish tradition. I smiled and cried at the same time. I saw her parents and her favorite aunt. I wondered if there was a Jack or two in the room. I learned later that there was.

After the ceremony, I attended a Seudat Hawra'ah – first meal – at the home of a good friend of hers. According to tradition, this is a meal after the funeral for all of the guests to ensure that her loved ones didn't neglect the care for their own bodies as they mourned. Miriam had told me about this too, so I wanted to be sure to attend. There were eggs, grapes, and bagels

— all were round to symbolize the circle of life. I made a point to eat everything round. I met her favorite aunt, who was lively, reflective, and delightful. She adored getting to meet Miriam's friends. The owner of the home seemed to know me from Miriam's stories, but I didn't remember hearing about her. I pretended I'd heard of her to be polite. I found some of our common friends and asked what had happened.

"I didn't know the end was so near," I said. "She didn't tell me, and I guess, I wasn't reaching out then either."

"Yeah, she told us not to tell you."

"Oh no." *Why?!*

"Well, she wanted to give you space to do your work. She knew your flow was important. She didn't want to bother you with her dying, especially since she didn't know how long she would live."

"I understand, but I wish she would have allowed me to be bothered. Honoring and supporting Miriam was no bother at all. She is…I mean was…such an amazing person."

And we all knew that.

Being Miriam's friend as she approached the end of her life taught me that knowing that you are dying can be a real gift, versus dying unexpectedly. Dying people have the opportunity to reprioritize, to live more intentionally. I hoped that if I ever received that news, that I was dying, that I could view it as a gift.

Miriam taught me how to live — to think less conservatively about the future, because it is uncertain after all. What is certain is now. Because of Miriam, I've made less rational purchases, I've said yes to adventuresome travel opportunities, and I look around and appreciate my present as much as I can remember to do.

I am alive. My health is great. I can breathe good air and drink clean water. I am happy.

Chapter 9

December 7, 2007

B y the time Miriam had died, I had learned that as scary as death, loss, and change are – they also bring opportunities for perspective and fresh starts. I reevaluated my life – my relationships, my job, and my priorities. I went through a lot of painful changes, yet I came through on the other side married to Dan and moving to Hawai'i for my tenure-track college faculty position.

Upon my move to Hawai'i at age 35, I had already experienced eight peer deaths. In addition to my freshman year suitemate, Chris, Shannon, Nick, and Miriam, I had also experienced the loss of a high school friend and neighbor who died with breast cancer, another high school friend who died in a country road accident, and my third ex – Brian. I had become certain that the deaths were a personal message to me. I felt called to process all of the deaths in a meaningful way, lest they continue.

I was beginning to work on a belief that my life was following a predetermined path. I saw that I was drawn to Chris because of my doubt in my own religion. My studying of the Bible with Jehovah's Witnesses led to my development of a complete distrust of religion and a deepening of my intellectual and rational pursuits. I saw my heartache from losing Chris as an opening for me to consider loving women. I saw my love of Shannon as a catalyst for deepening my empathy for other people. She suffered so much, even as she hurt me, and it was all understandable. Shannon's death taught me to pay attention to my limits of just how much of myself I would be willing to sacrifice to others. Experiencing the sudden and tragic deaths of Chris and Shannon prepared me for the slower deaths of Nick and Miriam. Nick's decreasing energy and hospitalization revealed to me my discomfort with death, and my self-centered concern that his emotional stability might depend on mine. My relationship with Miriam processed all of my fears and assumptions about dying. Miriam taught me to see dying as a gift, an opportunity to reprioritize life, purchases, decisions, and relationships.

All of these events seemed to be leading somewhere intentional. It felt as if it all happened not just *to* me, but *for* me. Death was all about me.

All the while I wondered what the message for me, personally, *was* in all of this experience with death.

To find out, I decided to intentionally spend my next birthday in mourning…at Pearl Harbor. I had an overwhelming calling to visit, as if life rolled out the precise set of circumstances for me to be there. I attended the 66th anniversary memorial event at Pearl Harbor with the hopes of a message being revealed to me.

Pearl Harbor would deliver.

I sat in my damp clothes, after having been doused by a mysterious stream of water during my water taxi ride to the ceremony venue. I was surrounded by rows and rows of strangers, mostly tourists, for the Pearl Harbor Day memorial ceremony. Speaker, singer, tribute, reflection, performance — on and on the event continued. I didn't mind. Toward the end of the event, our attention was directed out to the harbor behind the podium. We were to watch in silent reflection as a giant battleship, apparently one of a similar size to the USS Arizona, would cruise by. We were told that the crew would be saluting the survivors who were present at our event. *Oh, there are survivors here? Of course there are survivors here.* I was excited to see it. We waited for the ship to come on cue. When it finally came around the edge of the harbor and into view, it gave me chills. It was massive. As it came closer to our venue I could no longer see the top due to the roof of the pavilion blocking the full view. It moved quietly like a swipe across the background of the stage. It looked like a gracefully moving skyscraper. The decks, top to bottom, were lined with hundreds of sailors in 1940s-period service dress whites. They stood, saluting, perfectly still as they slipped by. The effect of their clean white uniforms against the solid dark grey ship was powerful. They were saluting the survivors who were with us. In the pavilion. At that moment. *They are here. I am among them.*

Next, readers read, one by one, the names of all those who died that day. For some names, the reader explained the person's job, what they had been doing that morning, and how exactly they were killed, if known. The names kept going and going.

Each story got to me. A private was swabbing the deck below and killed instantly. A cook was cleaning up the breakfast meal. I learned that my current senator, Daniel Inouye, was just a 17-year-old townie at the time, and he worked heroically to save as many people as he could. I sensed a shift in me.

These stories were all true, and they took place right here in front of me. And many of the people in this pavilion were there that day. It rocked their world. *They were being bombed. They know what that's like. They felt the sensation of complete insecurity of their steps and breaths. Which would be the last? This one? Or this one? But they survived, and they thanked their lucky stars that they did.* I even learned of some who had wished they *had* died that day. The day took their buddies, their confidence, their innocence, and they wanted to be down there with everyone else. This was *their* day. I was the impostor.

When the event was over, I walked slowly back to the line to the water shuttles. I didn't mind being on the last one out. I was mostly dry. I read every flower arrangement ribbon. I watched the band pack up.

I saw a veteran survivor holding a sign that was clearly made last year in honor of the 65th anniversary, though this year there was a 6 patched over where the 5 had been. He was here last year. *He might come every year. Pearl Harbor is* his *place. This is where his life changed forever.* A tear set in my eye and a lump in my throat. I wondered if he lived nearby, so that it is more convenient to come here. *I wonder if he volunteers here and gives tours. I wonder if he has a hard time saying goodbye to this place.* I understood — it's his place, not mine.

As I stared at this man, I had a crashing feeling of something that I already knew. *I am not special here. Pearl Harbor is not my place. It is not about me.*

None of this has ever been about me. I haven't died; I've never even faced my own mortality. How dare I feel proud of myself for being the person who knows death like a friend. It's never been my own. I've been looking through the glass window at the dying, with my nose pressed against the glass, feeling proud that I had these chances to know death.

I was reminded of Miriam's comments at Nick's memorial service, "This isn't about me. … I could bring my own story here and allow it to cloud all I see, but it's harder to experience life when it's filtered in that way. Right now, I am all about experiencing life as best as I can."

Somehow I had contorted that death was all about me, and it was suddenly clear to me now, it wasn't.

Through my instant perspective shift, Pearl Harbor was suddenly about the thousands whose lives were drastically changed that day, even my grandfather who would be drafted. Not to mention the identity of our whole nation, which realized we are not invincible. We are vulnerable; we are mortal. And this is all okay, this is the way things are supposed to be. As the realization that this wasn't about me sank in, I felt more at peace. *This is just…life.*

There is some comfort in believing that horrible things happen for a reason. Humans are drawn to the idea of a plan. That human suffering is not a punishment, but a calling. Humans rationalize that there must be a divine plan, because if there's not, life is terrifying. But to believe that some people are meant to suffer or die young, while some aren't, is just gross. To me, there seemed to be no justice in such a belief. And to believe so, in my case, felt too self-important. When I sat down to write this memoir, I believed that life simply *is* terrifying. And the belief that "everything happens for a reason" is a resistance strategy, to avoid dealing with the genuine suffering that is inherent in human life. The suffering and death just happen. There is no built-in, predetermined purpose.

I thought the end punchline would be, "NO, everything does *not* happen for a reason." Life is just random. It's not *ABOUT* me, or you or anyone. It's not specifically designed for any of us.

And that's how this book was going to end.

But that's not how this will end.

There were more lessons…via my experiences with loss…and death….

Chapter 10

Rebecca

S oon after settling into my new home in Hawai'i, and just one year after Miriam's death, I reconnected with an old college friend. Rebecca and I had been resident assistants, or RAs, together our senior year in college in the early 1990s. Back then, she was a born-again Christian, and I was coming out — though, not to her. I liked Rebecca a lot. She was a good friend, but I kept things between us light because I knew she'd judge me negatively if she knew me any better.

Her favorite TV show was *Tool Time*, and we'd watch that together in her room. Her best friend, Jill, was a little person – probably a bit over four feet tall – who I also enjoyed getting to know. Knowing Jill challenged me to think extra hard about what privileges I have with my height and how I should or shouldn't help my friend. I knew I should stop myself from thinking *Jill can't...fill-in-the-blank – play sports, be a leader, reach the sink* – and so on, but when she couldn't reach the silverware in the dining hall, I didn't help her and I felt sick about it. I waited for her to ask for my help, but she didn't. I stood there and waited, but she didn't ask. She reached and reached, but obviously wasn't going to get the silverware. She didn't even look at me. I figured that she came here every day. She knew what to do. A voice in my head screamed, *Don't assume she can't do this! Don't assume she needs your help!* So I walked away. I knew instantly after I'd walked away that that wasn't the right thing to do, but I didn't know what the right thing was to do. Days later it occurred to me that I could have asked her if she needed help, but...*but isn't that the same as assuming she needs the help?* I enjoyed the discomfort I felt around Jill. Being near her made me think hard. And then I felt badly that I thought of her that way, too, as a mental toy for me. *Ugh.*

Rebecca and Jill thought I was funny, so that made me want to try extra hard to get them to laugh. We had a fire alarm one day, and as RAs, Rebecca and I were in charge of clearing everyone out. Of course it was burnt microwave popcorn for the umpteenth time, so it was getting harder for folks to take things seriously. After a tough hour of work cajoling our peers and working with the local fire department, I headed to Rebecca's room to goof off and decompress.

I jumped to her open doorway wide-armed. "Ya know what you need to do in a fire, right?!" Jill was already there. They both looked at me as if to say, *What is she doing? Is she joking?*

"You gotta stop." I jumped into a wide-legged stance. "Drop," as I clunkily lay down on her floor on my back. "And roll," which I did, but it was harder on my body than I had imagined it would be.

They cracked up. "What was that?!"

"I don't know. It just came to me. I wanted to make you laugh." And that was our inside joke. They successfully begged me to do it a few more times that year. It was our thing. "Stop, drop, and roll."

Rebecca and I fell out of touch after college for a few years, but after email became more commonly used, we found each other and swapped occasional emails. Our opening exchange was about "stop, drop, and roll," and how she'd never forget that. And we continued to keep it light. Her updates included marriage, two kids, and church activities. Though my updates included moving in with same-sex partners and later break-ups with those partners, I only shared career updates and city moves. She must have thought I led a career-driven and lonely life.

The last update of myself that I gave her was in 2007 when I married Dan and moved to Hawai'i for a job. Her subsequent update trumped mine, such that our communications would no longer be about me at all anymore. They were just about her, and they were no longer light. These were intense exchanges now. Rebecca was the most vulnerable with me that she had ever been. I would never be in a position to return the favor.

She had a bizzaro cancer. It was nothing that the doctors could simply name and treat. Any approach taken would be a guess, an experiment — a "gosh, we hope this works. It seems like it might." I thought of Nick and his bizarre cancer. I thought of Miriam and her struggle. At that point in my life, I only knew one person who had survived cancer — my grandmother with her postmenopausal breast cancer. My experience to date was that most people I knew with cancer died. I thought, *here we go again.*

Rebecca was oddly optimistic. At first, her email updates were cautious. "We'll have to wait and see what the next doctor says." "So happy to be on a drug that seems to work. Time will tell." "Great news, I qualify for chemo!" Then her news got more and more discouraging. Didn't work. New tumors. Nausea. Can't be with the kids.

She and her husband decided not to tell the kids. With each new promising approach, Rebecca felt that she would survive, so why trouble her young children with something too scary that doesn't really affect them. I thought that was a mistake. *She doesn't have energy for them, and they need to know why. She is preoccupied and deeply sad, and they need to know why.*

Around that time I sat in on a talk about research that was going on at the University of Hawai'i where I was working. There was a local plant, noni, that was preliminarily testing well as a possible cure to cancer. I sent Rebecca a care package of Hawai'i noni lotion and other Hawaiian goodies.

A local friend of Rebecca's wanted to help her finish her scrapbooking projects that had been piling up. I'm sure this woman was thinking that if Rebecca dies, the scrapbooks are something she'll want to leave behind completed. She emailed all of Rebecca's address book friends and asked us for pictures, stories, and supplies, and for local people to help her and Rebecca put it all together. I sent in a picture from college and my stop, drop, and roll story. Oddly, I felt the advice for what to do when you are on fire was fitting for when you have cancer. Stop — deal with it, see it, don't deny it. Drop — get down, dirty,

and low with the emotions of it. Cry and share the grief. Roll —
let life take you where it needs you to go. Roll with it. Now is the
time. I felt Rebecca was so pleased with her pre-cancer life that
she was attempting to still live there. Resisting.

Rebecca seemed to have become a super mom, a good
Christian woman whose job was to raise her kids and support her
husband's career. Her family and her church were her life.

She wrote a mass email about the scrapbooks and how
grateful she was to have those done through the help of so many
people.

Then, one drug after another stopped working. A new
surgery option sounded promising, then it wasn't. As evidence
piled up toward the contrary, Rebecca firmly believed that she
would not die. She couldn't and wouldn't accept death as a
possibility. With each update she shared Bible verses that
comforted her. She shared inspirational lessons from her minister
who was visiting her daily.

She had become convinced that she would not die, that
the challenge now was to find the miracle that would ultimately
save her. Or perhaps God Himself would save her. What an
honor that would be for her to feel the hand of God deeply in her
life in that way. There were two key reasons why Rebecca was
convinced she would not die. First, she was entirely too faithful.
The minister explained that if she believed in God's plan, then she
would not be afraid. Trust in the Lord and you will survive. Good
comes to the faithful, for they deserve it. And, boy, was Rebecca
faithful, especially now. She couldn't allow in any doubt at all.
Second, Rebecca's two very young kids needed her too much. It
would not be possible for God's plan to remove Rebecca from her
kids. That would be too cruel for a loving God such as hers.

Although I believed very different things from Rebecca,
about God, life, death, and whether to include her kids in what
was happening, I understood that I should keep those feelings to
myself entirely. I only shared encouragement, but I kept it
authentic. I'd type, "thinking of you," "keep strong, Rebecca,"
"you are such an admirable fighter," and "my best to your family
in this difficult time." Her messages made it clear that the way to
support her through this was to help her believe what she needed
so badly to believe — it was a matter of life and death to her.

I started to receive bulk emails from Rebecca. Nothing was just for me anymore, other than the quick replies to my brief encouraging messages. The emails increased in frequency, once a month, once a week, daily.

Rebecca's update emails became more and more entrenched in this miracle belief. It seemed that Rebecca believed that if she allowed any doubt that she may not survive, then that's exactly what would happen — because doubting your god most certainly deserves the penalty of death. Rebecca continued to not tell her children. She made no plans for leaving the earth. She didn't tell her kids good-bye. She just died one day while waiting for her miracle.

One day in February 2008 I received an email from Rebecca's husband, and I instantly knew. It was over. That poor man. Those poor kids. I sent my condolences. That was not the way to die. That was not it.

I received the email while at work and immediately I put my face in my hands and sobbed. I knew it was coming; it was inevitable. But part of me wanted to believe, along with Rebecca, that the miracle would come. Once I gathered myself, I sat in the office of my supervisor. "Another death." She knew my history because I had taken my birthday off from work two months earlier to go to Pearl Harbor.

"I'm so sorry, Kelly. Are you okay? Do you need to go home?"

"No. No. I just need to think and talk. I feel so judgmental. It was Rebecca's life, her call, her reasons for how to handle things. But I think it was so wrong. Those kids lost their mom and didn't see it coming. No extra special anything from their dying mom. No hug, good-bye, special advice book for their teen years. What made this one so hard is that I learned exactly what I would never want to do if I were dying. And that makes me judgmental."

Though I had decided that these deaths weren't about me, I still sensed that lessons were presented in these circumstances. The contrast of the way Rebecca went about her death journey, as compared to Nick and Miriam, had me thinking, *What if I found out that I were dying? How would I approach it? Not like*

Rebecca, please. More like Nick or Miriam. I hoped. I hoped I wouldn't soon find out.

I rested my hand on my belly and looked down to my soon-to-be child. *I will want to be honest with you about death and loss, even if the truth is unbearable in the short term; in the long term we will both be stronger.* What I couldn't understand yet, is that my repeated experiences with loss were preparing me for motherhood.

Chapter 11

Peyton

[Note: This chapter describes the birth of my transgender son. Of course, at the time of his birth we couldn't know that he was transgender. We understand now that he was always a boy, even upon his birth. I want to honor two truths: the truth of what we know now and the truth of what we assumed then. As I tell this story, I'll refer to him as a girl, because that is how we understood the situation at that time (he approves of this choice). Additionally, I want to acknowledge here that he was always a boy.]

B y June 2008, my academic semester had wrapped up. Since I was on a nine-month contract, I had no pressing work to do. My preggo belly was large, and I was uncomfortable. All I could stand to do was lie down sideways and wait for the baby to come out. *Then I'd finally be comfortable.* I had no idea what was to come.

A few of my friends had experienced miscarriage and one even experienced a devastating still birth; I knew to remain guarded. *It is possible that my expectations of having a healthy live baby may be sidelined, and given my track record such a story could very well be my story.* I kept my excitement in check, though all signs were that we'd have a healthy baby.

According to my weekly pregnancy check-ups for three solid weeks, my cervix was three centimeters dilated and the fetal position was -3…ready to go! My belly regularly tightened up into a ball with no pain. We were hesitant to attend events across the island, wondering if we could make it back to the hospital in time if we had to. Labor almost started the week of our due date, but that was false labor. After another week of waiting, we decided to relax and have another adventure before we had a baby in tow. Dan and I spent a Saturday afternoon driving up the western Wainae Coast, swam at Yokohama Bay, and sunned our bellies on the secluded beach. We had a light dinner of kalua pork quesadilla and virgin lava flow cocktails at Ko'olina resort.

That night at 1:50 a.m. I woke as I usually did with my uncomfortably large body and unusually small bladder. I noticed some cramping but didn't think much of it. In the bathroom I was surprised to have diarrhea, though my body was doing a lot of weird things these days. Then the cramping happened again, but harder, and I knew it was time.

"Dan," I whispered loudly. I wanted to wake him but gently. I heard him roll over, then settle back down. Then pain surged with more diarrhea, this time harder.

"DAN!" I yelled.

"What!?" he jolted. He was annoyed.

"It's time!"

"What?"

"This is it. It's time."

"Let's go now," he jumped out of bed all a scramble, jittery hands grabbed for clothes.

"Call the doctor first," I said in a soft voice, followed by a pain induced grunt.

"No, we need to just go."

"But this could last for hours. Dr. Sun told us to call him first. Call the number."

"It's too late. We should get you right to the hospital," Dan said with certainty. I had no idea how right he was.

"I'm not sure how to get into a car, though," as I continued to have diarrhea with my contractions. "I don't think I'll make it without ruining our car."

"We can do this. We have to."

I doubled over with pain as Dan led me to our car. I sat on a stack of beach towels in the passenger seat. During our five-minute car ride, I hollered through two contractions, but no mess. Dan parked directly in front of the hospital entrance. A front desk worker swiftly pushed a wheelchair out to meet us. He instructed Dan to park the car then meet me on the second floor, as he took me up.

The first thing the triage nurse wanted to know was how long we waited before coming in. "Huh, wait? Um, well we didn't wait," I explained. "The pain started at 1:50." I looked at the clock, it was 2:05.

By the time she conducted her exam Dan had found me again. The nurse did a finger check, "Whoa, you are at nine centimeters!" She looked at Dan, "How long did you wait?" But he didn't hear her.

"Whoa really?" I said with surprise.

"What does that mean?" Dan had no idea.

"The baby starts coming at 10!" I explained. The reality was setting in for me. Dan's face lit up as he jumped softly in place and clapped. His excitement was not what I wanted to see. *Dude, this is going to be the hardest physical moment of my life. It's painful now, and it's about to get worse!* I looked back at the triage nurse.

She calmed her body with a deep breath, "We're going to take you directly to L&D. The good news is that we already called your OB. I'll call him back to let him know to come straight away."

The labor and delivery nurse was incredible. She held my feet, gave Dan ice chips to feed me, and helped me into my most comfortable position, on my hands and knees. She counted through my contractions so I would know they were temporary. But, the pain was too much.

"I need some relief. An epidural."

"Too late for that, dear," she said calmly.

"Some kind of local pain relief. Like, um, some drug that ends in -caine. Please!" I begged.

"Oh, no, no, too late for that," she repeated.

But I had read up on this and was prepared to be my own advocate. "It's a myth! No such thing, it's never too late. I can have it!"

She smiled, "Okay, yes, that's right, you can have it. But it takes an hour to kick in, and by then your baby will already be born and have the drug in its body, too. Are you sure that's what you want?"

The news caught me off guard, but made sense. "Are you serious? I have to do this? This is too hard. I can't do this!"

"Oh yes, you can. Look at that clock, your baby will be born in 30 minutes. Watch the clock, you can do this," she said convincingly. The clock read 3:45 am. I had already been doing this for nearly two hours. "And it feels better to push through the contractions, so you only have a few more moments of these contractions."

Dr. Sun arrived to see me on my hands and knees taking each contraction with agony. "I can't do this!" I screamed at him.

"You can do this," he responded calmly.

"I can't," I argued. And rather than engage, he turned to the nurse to get my updates. He went back into the hallway as the nurse coached me through several more contractions.

"Focus on the in-between," she said slowly "the calm, not the storm. Be sure you are resting when you can." And she continued to count down the time during contractions. This proved to be excellent life advice, too, though I was becoming better at focusing on the calm *inside* the storms. "Five...four...three...two...one. Rest."

When it was time for pushing, Dr. Sun came back in. "Okay, I need you to turn over," he instructed.

"What?! Are you kidding me? I can't move. I'm trying to get through this pain. I can't do anything else," I tried to reason with him as another contraction hit me. "This is better for me. I can do it this way."

He talked to the nurse, then went to the hallway again.

"You are going to be able to do better delivery pushes if you are on your back," the nurse said with a calming voice, "you can curve your body in a circle so the baby comes out easier."

"I can make a circle like this," I arched my back. "This is just fine. And it's actually better because gravity is on my side." I couldn't believe I needed to advocate for myself in this most compromised situation. "He just doesn't want to have to bend down. Look at me here!" as I wildly gestured to my entire body. "Why does his convenience matter more than mine?!"

Dan got concerned, "Kell-EE" he said with a shaming voice, "Do what the doctor says."

The nurse added, "I think you want your OB to have the best angle possible to deliver your very slippery child."

How did she always know the right thing to say?

The nurse helped me to time my flip between two contractions. And the next one came as soon as I was in place on my back and in the stirrups. No rest for the weary this time.

The nurse led me through some initial pushes, and she was right. The pain didn't hit quite so hard when I could push with the contraction. It took me a while to figure out where to push. I pushed through my vagina.

"This next time, push like you're going to poop."

"Through my butt? But something will come out."

"Actually, it almost always does. Go ahead. Let it out."

This was no place for decency.

Dr. Sun came back in to rupture my sac and to begin the final pushes.

"You'll feel a gush of warmth wash over you." And I did.

"Oh, wow, that actually feels really good," I said.

Dr. Sun smiled at me. Then shortly after he and the nurse shared some excitement and whispering. "Um, okay, we have a very small complication," Dr. Sun explained in a clear voice.

Oh shit.

"This is very common," he assured us. "There's meconium in your sac. Basically, Baby pooped," he said with a smile. "Our concern is that Baby not breathe it. We can deal with it if that happens, but it's much easier if there's no aspiration. You just need to do what I say exactly when I say."

I calmed and was on board. My amateur website-based birthing knowledge had come to its limit. At this point I could have panicked. A "complication" with my baby is certainly grounds for logical fear. But it didn't register that way. Perhaps by this time in my life, I had already been trained to save my fears and worries for the moment when they are called for. The more I experienced loss, the smaller that window of time became – *Is it time to panic now? No. What about now? No.* Or maybe my brain was too preoccupied by the present birthing process to sit in my fears for the future. Either way, I was poised.

"What I'll need to do is have you push slowly. We need to wipe and suction baby's mouth and nose before the first breath. I need to do this as soon as the mouth and nose emerge, and I need you to not push at that point." He paused and looked at the ceiling to gather his thoughts. "Got it? I'm going to ask you to do a half-push, stop for a while — despite you having the urge, you're going to have to hold it. Then you can push again when I tell you."

"Got it," I was ready to do as I was told.

A few more pushes and the nurse and Dan started chatting. "Do you see the head?"

"Where? Um, no," Dan had been reluctant to look, afraid of seeing my pain.

"Look here," the nurse pointed. "I see red hair!"

"Oh, I see. I see," and just like that Dan was delighted. "Red hair!"

"Okay here comes Baby," Dr. Sun said sharply interrupting the chatter. The room got quiet. He looked me directly in the eyes, "Listen to me. Push hard on this one, but stop and hold it when I tell you." He turned his full attention back to the birth. I pushed as hard as I could. "Stop," he said firmly.

Swift movements ensued in my crotch area.

"Ow, ow, ow, ow," I begged as I realized that Baby's head was stopped at the opening of my vagina. My body was open the widest that it had ever been, and it was going to have to stay there. I looked to Dan for help, but his bright face revealed he was too engrossed in witnessing the birth of his child.

"You're doing great. Hold it. You can do this," Dr. Sun encouraged me. "Okay, ready? Let's push again."

"Oh thank God!" I exhaled.

"It's a girl!" The nurse announced to a now crowded room. "A red-headed girl!"

Congratulations and cheers filled the room, as Dan announced her name, "Hello, Peyton Jo Merrill" – a family name that honored both sides of her family.

I caught a glimpse of her slimy yellow-tan body between my legs as she was whisked away to the back corner of the L&D room.

She's here, and our lifetime together has just begun.
I looked at the clock, 4:20 am.
What is today? It's her birthday. Sunday, June 22. Good, not a death day.
"You did a great job holding her there." Dr. Sun stayed with me as nearly everyone else in the room followed Peyton to the corner. "I think we got her nose and mouth all clean," Dr. Sun explained. "The team is going to do a thorough cleaning now. But I think everything went just fine."

I watched the activity in the back room without making a special effort to lean or move for a better view. I was too exhausted for that. Peyton was brought to me wrapped up in hospital issue blankets. She was calm and awake. I was fully aware that I was holding my baby for the first time.

You and me, Peyton, we're in this for the long haul. We are finally together. Only you know who you are, and I look forward to getting to know you. Who knows what life will bring us? But I'm ready to do it with you. With time, the lessons I would learn from this one child's life would rival the lessons I had learned through my proximity to death.

I studied her face, her nose, her skin. I watched her eyes decide if they should notice mine. Her eyes were wide open, glassy, and dark. She studied everything: the ceiling, my shoulder, the wall. Her cone-shaped head, formed from the squeeze of birth, was covered with a knit pink beanie. Peyton was not only adorable; she was already obviously intelligent. I held her for some pictures, trying unsuccessfully to get both her face and mine in the same shot.

"Thank you for working so well with me." I apologized to Dr. Sun. "I'm sorry for my belligerence."

"Oh, well," he chuckled. "That was pretty amazing on your part. I mean that was very painful."

"Well, probably no more painful for me than for anyone else."

"Um, not quite. Because you delivered so quickly," he looked at the clock. "Um, when did you feel your first pain?"

"At 1:50."

"So," he calculated as he looked at the ceiling, "that's two and a half hours!" He looked back at me, "Whoa. Yeah, because she came that quickly, you didn't have time to build up to the pain. You went from little pain to full pain so fast. Like 0 to 60. You did great, though."

"Really? So it hurt worse for me?"

"Kinda, yeah, just the build-up makes the pain more possible to manage, but when you don't have that...so yeah, I'm impressed."

"Well, it wasn't my choice. I didn't want to do it with the pain. I was chicken."

"You did great."

"I'm sorry I yelled at you."

"Oh, that was nothing. I've seen much worse, and we're used to it. We know how to work through it. Delivering a healthy baby is the focus."

"Well...well done. Thank you. You were perfect."

At home, motherhood was harder than I anticipated. I knew sleepless nights were ahead, but I didn't quite grasp the impact of every single night being interrupted. Being able to crash for at least a solid day, as I had been able to do after final exam week in college, wouldn't happen until years later. And I knew that breastfeeding meant that I'd have to feed every couple of hours, but I didn't understand how this would feel day after day. My body also wouldn't produce enough milk to get my baby through a few hours; we'd be feeding every hour. I knew that babies slept a lot and not in solid chunks of time. I didn't realize that the sleep was easily interrupted by a slight noise or jostle, that if she fell asleep while I held her, which often happened during feedings, that I would feel compelled to not move for the next several hours. I wouldn't be able to go to the bathroom, get a snack, or entertain myself with a book or TV if the resources were out of reach. Before having a baby, I thought the genius strategy would be to sleep when the baby slept. But when the baby happened to sleep in her bassinet, there was too much to do to sleep. Like walking, reading, stretching, eating, peeing — let alone the laundry, dishes, food prep. Responding to notes, calls, and gifts of congratulations was entirely out of the question.

While I sat holding the feeding baby near constantly, Dan saw me as being lazy and not contributing to all that had to be done in the house. He never told me this. I eventually figured it out by reading his non-verbal cues and snarky interactions with me. Dan would grudge-clean the house around me as if I should be the one doing the cleaning. As if me sitting and holding or feeding the baby was the same as me being lazy. When I finally realized what he was thinking, I raged on him hard.

"I hate just sitting here. I hate being sucked on every hour. I feel trapped," I said through streaming tears. "My body is not my own, and it hasn't been for months. I hate watching you get to go to work, while I do all of this alone. I hate hearing you say how much you'd rather be home with the baby. Is that supposed to make me feel better?! Because it feels like a God damn guilt trip! That you notice that I'm not loving every moment of this, and that you judge me for it. This 'sitting here' stuff is WORK. It is hard, exhausting work. And you cannot do it for me. I have to do this. And I could sure use not only your help with a smiling-face around the house, but also your admiration and awe for me for doing what I'm doing every God damn moment of every God damned day. AND NIGHT!"

Maybe he got it. Maybe he just saw me as a complainer. Maybe he continued to judge me but extended forgiveness due to the situation. Who knows? I mean, he was sleep-deprived, too, after all. Whatever he thought of my explosion, he started to do chores with a happy face as I continued to just sit there.

Two weeks into motherhood, my mother came to visit. In addition to meeting her first grandchild, she was eager to help.

Finally consistent relief is here!

"I want to do housework for you," she explained. "The dishes, laundry, and meals...all of that. As much as I want to hold my granddaughter, I want to maximize your time with her. I want you to hold her and get to sleep."

"Mom that sounds great, but more than anything, I really want you to hold her so that I can stand up and walk around. And I want to pee when I want to."

"Oh, sure. Whatever you need. I would love to hold her."

"And the sleep, yes, the sleep sounds great. Does that go for nights, too?"

"Oh, no, I guess not that part." And she giggled with a supportive squeeze of my arm. "You and Dan can be in charge of that part."

"Well, I'm the only one with the boobs, so it's just me... And it's me all day...and all night. All the time. I would love to sleep, but I haven't figured out how to sleep and feed Peyton at the same time."

"Can you sleep in between?"

"You mean the 20 minutes in between? She can't get enough to eat to last much more than that, because I don't make enough. That small break is when I pee and get a snack — that is, if she's not asleep on me." I was so fried. All I could think about was what I was not getting that I needed so desperately, and there was no end in sight of the deprivation. I was reminded of the lesson that I learned with Shannon; I have limits to how much of myself I am willing to give up to others – even to people I love. At this point, it felt as if I had given up all of me.

"We'll do what we can. We'll find a way. You've got me now." I had always known my mother to be an excellent problem-solver.

We found opportunities for new routines. Mom and I went on morning walks every day. I'd strap Peyton into a front carrier and we'd walk back into the Manoa Valley to a Chinese cemetery. Each visit we'd notice something new — offerings of fruit and flowers left at certain sites, birth and death dates, family relations, and preparations for new burials. A row upfront was made up entirely of babies who had died before their first birthdays. There is a tradition in Hawai'i that the first birthday party is a large luau celebration. I was told that this tradition dates back to the high infant mortality rates on the islands before institutionalized healthcare arrived, and here was the evidence of such a time. Mom and I'd walk through the cemetery making up stories about the relationships of the people here, about what circumstances finally took each life. I looked at my mother and knew she'd have an end one day. That I would too. And eventually Peyton. Even this cemetery wouldn't be here forever. I treasured our time together in this space. At the back end of the cemetery park, we turned to look back from the direction we had come. Before us was a stunning view out of Manoa Valley, of the

Waikiki skyline and the ocean behind. *Look at that amazing view. We are all three lucky to be right here right now in this calm spot that so happens to be in the middle of a storm.*

Mom helped me to get Peyton to nap in the crib more often. We noticed her natural patterns for naps and made sure she was in a crib for those times. I was able to take a daytime nap in my own bed that lasted so long that I woke on my own two hours later. Mom did all of the house chores. I loved her being there.

When my dad came to visit I told him that motherhood was hard work.

"I didn't appreciate how dependent a baby is," I confessed. "I'm doing everything for her, so much that what I need to do for myself gets compromised." Each day continued to serve as a reminder of what I had learned by giving too much of myself in my relationship with Shannon. "I wonder what's going to happen to me over time."

Dad knew what I was saying. He recalled that feeling, too. He gave me the best insight that I heard yet.

"Every day she will become more and more independent."

"Yeah, I know," I said dismissively.

"No," Dad shook off my dismissiveness. "Every day. Soon she'll eat from a bottle. Then she'll hold her own bottle. She will figure out how to sleep on her own. Every day comes with some new thing she can do all on her own. And it just goes on and on. It never stops. You are 35 and you are still learning new things." He smiled at me with awareness of my learning in this moment. This observation was where I found relief in those tough early days.

"That's good. Yeah, that makes sense," I said as it sank in.

"Every day comes with more relief," he emphasized.

"Yes, I guess I just didn't realize how dependent she would be. But I see now. Boy this is hard," I exhaled with an acceptance of the present state.

"No one can really prepare you for it. But it doesn't last forever." But, my loss of independence persisted and began to challenge my feeling of worthiness and eventually my identity, as if I was dying from the inside out.

Chapter 12

Career

My maternity leave plan had originally been to get publication manuscripts written during this time. I was so naive. Back when I was pregnant, I found it difficult to be productive with my writing. Sitting up in my desk chair was difficult, as my ribs dug into my uterus and I couldn't get enough air in my lungs while sitting up. The fatigue and nausea were real, too. Despite the discomfort, I had been successful at proposing, writing, and presenting conference papers, but I hadn't yet submitted a manuscript for publication. I had visions of being able to get that done once I was no longer pregnant. I had figured with a sleeping baby I would be able to finally write seated at my desk. And I'd have plenty of time. In addition to my summer off, I arranged for a reduced teaching load for fall term, teaching one evening class, to ease back into work with my then two-month-old.

My plan was not doable in the way I had envisioned and only partially doable with exorbitant support from others. My mom's visit helped me to finally breathe, get a little sleep, and discover a routine that made surviving possible. Once she left, I depended on Dan's support to allow me to get work done, but I didn't tell Dan explicitly of my plans.

On Dan's work days, even before he was awake for the day, my mornings began with feeding and then a walk with Peyton; afterward I would feed her again and put her down for a morning nap. I napped too, to attempt to catch up from the sleep I did not get at night. On the best days she could nap two hours, but I couldn't sleep that long. Not when it was daylight outside and things had to be done. I'd sit at my desk with my foggy brain and try to write my manuscripts and to prepare for my weekly class. I had so few moments to look at a computer that often all of my writing time went towards responding to emails. But even that got to be a challenge. A few times I would sit at the computer with Peyton in my lap. I could read fine, but typing was only possible in increments — a word or two at a time. Lunch was followed by activity and another at-best two-hour nap. Whenever Peyton was awake, she required stimulus and activity, despite my utter exhaustion and my long to-do list, and if she didn't get it, she would fuss. I tried to create situations where she would get her stimulation from something other than me. The baby "gym," a play mat with dangling toys and mirrors above it, only held her attention for 20 minutes tops, then the fussing would ensue. The excersaucer, a sit-in toy, also held her attention for 20 minutes. Baby Einstein videos lasted 30 minutes. These were not helpful time chunks for working — maybe for stretching, bathroom, and snack breaks, but not for the deep thinking of scholarly writing. And Peyton let it be known she preferred stimulation from people.

After a long day of being alone with Peyton, I looked forward to Dan getting home from work. I'd fantasize about leaving the house and going for a walk on my own. Then I could head to my office on campus for two hours to get some work done. But I soon learned that leaving Dan home alone with the baby was hard on him. He would say the right things, "Okay, have a great night in class," but his hands would tremble with doubt. One night when I taught my evening class, Dan called and left me a cellphone voice message, except that it wasn't him talking. I heard Peyton crying for over a solid five seconds, then Dan's sarcastically positive voice, "Um, come home as soon as you can."

YOU ARE A FUCKING PARENT, TOO. YOU DO THIS! WHAT MAKES YOU THINK I'M ANY BETTER AT THIS THAN YOU?! Do NOT try to make me feel bad for getting a little space, a tiny sliver of me-time. And REALLY, I don't think that me getting to go to work for two hours one day a week gets to count as me-time! I kept those thoughts to myself.

I arrived home and Dan was trying to put Peyton into a counter-top bathtub as she wailed. Upon seeing me he quickly held Peyton out toward me. I held her and she stopped crying immediately.

"See? See! She'll calm down for you. Only her mommy will do!" Dan was so fried.

"No," I shook off his claims. "I'm not better at this than you. It's just as hard for me." I tried to make my case as he looked at me with insistent eyes that pointed at Peyton's calm body.

"Kelly, this was not the worst of the evening. She bawled so hard she was red. There was nothing I could do. For hours it was like that!"

"Hold out your hands," I demanded. He held them out as they shook out of control. "You know, she can feel your energy." Dan looked like I punched him in the stomach. "She's responding to you. This isn't about me...or her."

Eventually Dan got into his groove and his class-night evenings with Peyton ran more smoothly. He made up giggle games with Peyton and new routines just for the two of them. My fantasies about leaving the house to work in my office seemed more realistic.

One day when Dan came home from work, I was ready to head out. I had my backpack packed with all of the supplies and resources I needed for manuscript writing. Dan walked in the door, and after our initial greetings he asked, "Can you take Peyton out of the house tonight? Like for a little walk and maybe even go out to dinner together? I want to work on my dissertation." Dan had been close to finishing his PhD, "all but dissertation," for two full years now, despite my suggestions that he should get it done before we had children.

I looked at him in shock. *Huh? Are you insane?*

"Well, I don't know," Dan shrugged, "Whatever you two want to do. Library? I just want to get to work on my dissertation again."

"Now?"

"Yeah, I really got to thinking about it today and I need to get this done while Peyton is small."

I agreed, but...but... *No, dude. No. You had your chance. You made your choice. The time has passed.*

"Um, really? But I need…" My voice was soft and trailed off. Now I was the one who felt a gut-punch.

"Yeah, it'll be great. I don't think I'm that far from getting this done. Just a couple of evenings should do it." Now he was feeding back to me past pep talks I had given him…before there was a baby.

Why does all of this make sense to you now? Why now? It's…it's too late.

"Can't you find time at work?" I searched for an alternative.

"Oh, I wouldn't do that. Work time is for work."

"But couldn't you consider it professional development?" *Please.*

"I wouldn't want to seem distracted from the office work."

Oh, I see. You won't compromise your job, but your wife is another story…she's expendable. She'll understand.

Am I out of my mind? Am I being too sensitive? "You know I've been home alone with Peyton all day. I kinda need a break." My eyeballs felt hot, even on the back sides, as I fought my tears.

"Oh, I would appreciate this favor very much," he dug-in as he reached out to hug me close. "This is temporary, just a couple times," he tried to assure me. But I knew this wasn't true. I was an experienced dissertator and now a dissertation adviser. At best this would be months of "favors"…the precise number of favors that I wanted to ask for from him.

What happened next would later become a source of deep resentment in my life, and simultaneously the spark to an entirely new and positive direction.

I put Peyton in her stroller and walked through the neighborhood. I had no idea where I wanted to go, and I had no idea how long I'd be gone. I brought the fully stocked diaper bag and car keys just in case. I didn't want to walk at all. I wanted to sit on the curb and cry, just like the exhausted and injured person that I was. But Peyton needed to keep moving. So I walked slowly.

What do I do?

I hoped for quick clarity. That the right words would find me soon enough that I could return back to the house and tell Dan, *No! This is my time. You stay here with Peyton. I'm leaving.* But I wanted to allow for the possibility that what he asked for might be the right thing to do. I wanted to stay close to the house, with the option to be near or go far.

I didn't even know what to think. I just walked. Stunned.

How is he even asking this of me? Doesn't he see me disappearing?

I walked farther into the valley. The breezes came down from the mountains and blew my hair as we strolled.

Do I tell Dan that I had plans to write? That he should support my plans to write instead of me supporting him? Do I tell him that his goals don't get to matter anymore? At least not for the next five years of my tenure process? Is there a compromise? Can we do both?

But I knew that any sliver of time I could find in my life already felt so precious. I struggled to find time to use the bathroom, to even type an entire email in one sitting. Meanwhile Dan went to his job every day and was able to do it without anyone sucking on his nipple as he composed emails or screaming at him if he didn't pay attention. I had no more time to compromise. None. I had already given my all.

As I walked deeper into the valley, it welcomed me further in. At each intersection I had to make a decision whether to wind myself back toward our home, or to keep walking farther in. Each time I had no more insight, just more complicated thoughts. I opted to go deeper into the valley.

Damn it! I told him this would happen! I told him to write in Chicago. I told him to write when I was pregnant. His turn is over!

But did I really tell him? No, I only politely suggested. I asked him questions, and hoped he would see. He did not see. I trusted him. I thought there was something I didn't see. I trusted that he knew himself. He didn't.

OH! I cannot change the past. That is all in the past. We are here now. What do I do now?!

I could feel the thud of my feet throughout my whole body as the valley welcomed me deeper. I still felt pulled backward.

I want so badly to change the past. Back in Chicago I would have said, "Write NOW, or I will not be able to support your dissertation writing ever again. This is me supporting you now. Not later when the burden is significantly heavier for me. NO, you do not know yourself better than I do. You do NOT. You need to write NOW, because there won't be time later." Because that would have gone over well. Ugh. Um...okay, so this isn't getting me anywhere.

What's the situation now?

What happens if I don't write now? If I don't get the writing done that I need to do, I will lose my job, not immediately, but within a couple years. And losing a tenure-track job makes getting another one very difficult. My career could be over.

If Dan doesn't write....well, he won't lose his job! But...it would hold back his career. He won't have as much career advancement potential as I would. And that would affect both of our livelihoods. Is that right? Maybe he would just be equal to me. A woman with a PhD is just as financially valuable as a man with a...what? A master's? Dang, maybe even a bachelor's. This whole line of thinking has me feeling so worthless.

Why not just pack up my career entirely? Why did I even get a PhD? If I can't even keep the job that comes with it, why did I even do it? Am I exaggerating?

Would I really lose my job? That certainly would be possible. Could I make up for the lost time? Maybe. Maybe not. Would my department understand if I couldn't? Maybe. I've seen other new mothers on the tenure track get allowances from their departments. But would mine extend understanding? Does mine like me enough to work with me through this? I would hope so, but it's a risk. Would my department see young motherhood as a temporary challenge? Is it a temporary challenge? Does this only get harder? This can't be any harder. It really can't.

I arrived at a local park, but decided to keep walking deeper into the valley. I didn't want to stop and run the chance that Peyton would fuss and cry. That would be the last thing my fragile emotions could take in this moment. I was one baby-cry away from a complete breakdown, right in the valley streets. I turned deeper, this time toward the Chinese cemetery creating a zig-zag path across the valley. Clarity might wait for me there; it had before. And it did.

Could one of us wait? Could we take turns? I have a tenure clock on me, so no...I can't wait. And yeah...Dan could revisit his "all but dissertation" status later, but there's probably a point at which he'd need to start over or at least reevaluate his progress. He has time constraints, too. And Dan's motivation to complete his dissertation has been shy. He wants to do it now. Asshole.

And my productivity is already compromised, even without supporting Dan! If I get Dan's complete support to write now, is there any guarantee that I'll get tenure? Not at all! Being a new parent is compromising my productivity enough. But also supporting his writing at home? I mean why not? I won't be productive anyway! What's the difference between writing a half-article and no article? None.

Do I tell Dan that I'm having these thoughts? Can I get his help deciding on a plan? Or is this all mine to decide? No, Dan should not get a voice in how much of me I allow to compromise. And wouldn't telling him about it only make him feel guilty about it? But damn it, he SHOULD feel guilty about this! Ugh, again, not helping.

Dan with a PhD would be a valuable thing for our family, not just for him. If he has the motivation to do it now, then so be it. I should support him in that. I HAVE a PhD. Why should I hold him back from getting his? As cool as it is that we were married as "Mr. and Dr. Merrill," I think I should support him to be a Dr., too. There are just too many unknowns as to how not writing will affect my career.

I arrived at the Chinese cemetery, the place where I first started to feel nature again after giving birth. This is where the sun hit my skin and my legs moved beneath me for my morning walks with Mom and Peyton. The cemetery had come to represent not just a calm spot in the storms of my life, but a reminder that sometimes life just unpredictably sucks. We can make all of the calculated decisions that we want, but circumstances beyond our considerations are a constant force of life. John Lennon's words came to mind, *"Life is what happens to you while you're busy making other plans."* As I faced the cemetery, I knew I was at a crossroads between my plans and my life. *Will this be a time for me to set up boundaries, or a time for me to accept the circumstances of life?*

I debated walking into the cemetery for more reflection, but I knew I already had my decision and that I needed to head home. My walk had lasted over an hour, and by the time I would get home it would be the full two hours that Dan had asked for.

When I returned Dan was glowing and appreciative. "Oh, thank you so much. That was really helpful. I got a lot done."

I laughed. I may have played it off as a happy-to-help laugh, but really it was a rage laugh. I had a flash vision of him blowing the time I had just given him — of him sitting down to type just as stuck as he's ever been when he worked on his dissertation, playing solitaire games to help him "mentally relax."

Oh, dude. You better get a lot done. You better. If I'm out there on the edge of sanity while you're here playing solitaire games...I do NOT care if it's helping you get into the right frame of mind. I absolutely do NOT care. I am giving you something extremely valuable. Do NOT squander it.

But instead I said, "I'm glad it helped." I wanted to cry. And yell. And mostly...I wanted to sleep.

"It did. It did. Thanks again," Dan tried to assure me.

I wanted to be honest about my feelings without laying guilt on him. I did my best.

"Look, I want you to know that I'm supporting you through this. But I want you to know it is very hard on me," and I started to cry through my voice. "The last thing I have is more energy to support you, but somehow I'm going to find it somewhere. I really do want you to have a PhD. You, of all people, deserve it."

All Dan could hear was that I was going to support him. He didn't hear my pain. "I really appreciate it, Kelly. I really do. I'll get this done as fast as I can. And I'll appreciate your feedback on my drafts. You always have good observations."

I drew the line, "No, I think I've given you enough feedback. Besides you need to concentrate on what your adviser tells you. She's the one who matters."

Dan worked hard and finally graduated in May 2009.

My decision to support Dan's writing marked the beginning of a deep loss for me, not just my career, but my identity. The loss threw into question my own sense of value in the world. Being a mother meant that my ambition to contribute to my profession became significantly challenged. In part this was due to simply being a mother (not just a parent, but a female parent, and all of the social expectations that go with that), but also it was due to my child's desperation to eventually become *him*self against social forces conspiring against him. My first child would eventually come out as transgender at age 10, which in hindsight offered explanation, but not relief, for those challenges. Again, I would feel that I had to say good-bye to a version of someone I deeply loved, but who was not quite gone. My experience with death familiarized me with the path of grief, but it took me years to understand that those same lessons would also apply to these other losses in my life.

Chapter 13

Liko

By 2009, our toddler was a blessing, but I was committed to not raising an only child, as I had been quite lonely as an only child myself. When Peyton was just over a year old, we began trying for a second child and were lucky to conceive on our third try. Given my academic life as a professor, I wanted my due date to give me as much time during my summer months as possible. Ideally I'd be due in April, May, or June. By July much of the summer break would be past, and I'd need to be back to work in just one month for the fall term. My second child was due June 13, 2010.

The first few weeks of pregnancy left several marks of concern, but each seemed to resolve. First, my pregnancy hormone levels remained so low that my pregnancy wouldn't register on pee sticks for quite some time. Second, my OB confirmed the pregnancy but was concerned that the low hormone levels and the small size of the embryo – in light of its age – could be a warning for miscarriage. He even wondered if the age of the embryo might actually be younger than we thought. It wasn't. At just six weeks pregnant I spotted nearly all day for two days straight. The OB explained that it was either the early warning signs for a miscarriage that would happen in about a week, or a reaction from my earlier vaginal ultrasound. But it passed without event.

Some of our child-bearing friends introduced us to the trend of in-utero names. Naming your embryo-slash-fetus something clever or cute meant that you could talk freely about your soon-to-be child without having to call it "it," "the baby," or feeling the need to officially name the kid before being born. Our friends named theirs Bump, Nut, Bean, Belzer, Baby-Clown (BC for short), or even Zozo (Voltaire's childhood nickname). We loved the idea. Just as soon as the idea occurred to us, we knew the name would have to be Hawaiian. We bought a book of Hawaiian names and discovered that many names were unisex, which worked perfectly, because with our first, we didn't want to know the baby's sex. We chose Ipo (Ee-po) for our first-born, meaning sweetheart, and for our second pregnancy we chose Liko (Lee-ko), meaning descendant.

Though we knew we were pregnant in October, we were committed to keeping our secret until we could tell our families in person during our holiday visits in December. Our family of three from Hawai'i visited my mother and her husband in Indianapolis. Dan's parents came to Indianapolis from Pittsburgh to visit with us. My beloved grandma came from northern Indiana to visit for Christmas Day. At 15 weeks pregnant, I was useless — tired, hungry yet full, vaguely nauseated, and easily annoyed. I was relieved to tell the family our news. They were all thrilled to learn we were pregnant again, this time with Liko.

From Indiana, we phoned my dad and our other two living grandmothers. We put the news in our annual holiday letter to 100 family and friends. After the holidays, I was free to tell my work, and began planning my 50% leave plan for the fall term. By the turn of the new year in 2010, everyone who mattered in our lives knew.

Dan and I had agreed that we'd ideally like to have a girl and a boy, "one of each." We knew that our children would be whoever they wanted to be, but there must have been enough residual gender-bias messages in our heads, not to mention transgender naiveté, that we bothered to have some sort of preference. For our first-born's 20-week ultrasound we said, "no thanks," when the technician asked if we wanted to know the sex. But for our second, we wanted to know. We figured, if we want one of each, the first one wouldn't matter, but the second would. We definitely had a preference this go around. As we understood gender at the time, we thought we had our girl, so this time we hoped for a boy. If we were going to have a second girl, we rationalized, we wanted to know earlier, so that we could be completely on board by the time she was born. Her name would be Mary Ann after my beloved grandmother. I could get behind that, to raise a girl named Mary.

We headed into our ultrasound at 19 weeks, on Friday, January 22, 2010, after Martin Luther King weekend. We would be traveling to Maui that weekend for a trip with close friends to celebrate Dan's 40th birthday. Many folks think of this ultrasound visit as the one when you learn your baby's sex, so our friends were excited to celebrate the news with us in Maui. But I knew the exam was about the baby's health and news of the sex was a convenient bonus. Way back in the depths of my mind, I did worry about the baby's health. *Why did the pregnancy take so long to test positive? Was this child meant to miscarry earlier and never did? Why was I so nauseated and cranky, so much more than my first pregnancy? And I am 38, after all.* I listened carefully to our technician as she walked us through the exam. She told us what she was looking at — heartbeat, foot, butt, and head. She took a lot of pictures, especially in one spot in particular. But she was careful not to use words like, "Looks good" or "healthy baby" as our tech had said with our first pregnancy. I figured this one must be more experienced and professional. She asked, "Do you want to know the sex?" I could sense something guarded in her question. "Yes," we both answered certainly. She turned the monitor to us and showed us some grey masses and lines that she explained were two hips and thighs with a penis poking out from in between. "A boy."

Dan wanted to be sure he had heard right, "It's a boy?!" And I heard a smile on the other end of his question. Otherwise, I heard caution in the room from our technician. I was tickled at his joy, but I touched his wrist. "I know. I know," he said and I thought he understood. "I should be happy either way, but it's a boy!!" he said as he attempted to whisper his enthusiasm.

"No, I mean she hasn't said anything about his health yet," as I checked the tech's face. She looked at me plainly.

"Yes, I'll bring the doctor in for the interpretation," and she left. While she was gone, I worried and tried to temper Dan's obvious excitement without killing his mood.

Doctor Ben Brooks was our prenatal diagnostician. He seemed about our age, maybe a bit younger. He had bushy, sandy-blonde hair and a cleft palate scar, if you stopped to notice. He walked in and spoke softly to the technician.

Feeling no patience, I interrupted their discussion and said boldly, "So, how do things look?"

"Most things are looking great," Dr. Brooks responded without hesitation. "There's just one concern, in the brain."

Trying to keep things light, I joked, "The brai-ain? Why not the foot? Really, the brain?"

"Yes, you're right, the brain can be serious, but we don't know that yet in your case. Here, let me confirm these measurements." And he was careful to show and educate us. "There are two symmetrical ventricles of fluid in the brain, and a type of circulatory system that moves the fluid over the brain and spinal cord then back to the ventricles again. See this large black area?" He used a mouse to click a tag mark on the edge of the black where he initiated one end of a line. "These ventricles are measuring much larger than they should for normal development." Then he dragged the line to the other side of the black mass, and got a reading of 18 millimeters. "And each time I try this from various angles, and on the other ventricle, 16 to 18 millimeters are the best measurements that I can get. That's in the severe category, anything 15 and over is severe. This is called ventriculomegaly."

"Oh wait, I want to write this down. What is it called?" Then he spelled it out.

"It just means enlarged ventricles, and many abbreviate it VM.

"Fetal diagnostics is a relatively new field – only about 40 years old – beginning when these ultrasound viewing technologies came on the scene, and they are always improving. Our knowledge of what these measurements mean is not extensive. We know that mild cases of VM, ten to eleven millimeters, are likely to resolve by birth, and have little to no manifestations. But that's not you. You're in the severe range. It's likely that your son will have some sort of disability, anywhere from a mild-to-severe mental disability. What we know of the prognosis of severe cases is so limited, because many chose to terminate." He paused. *Termination?!*

Is it time to panic now? No.

Dr. Brooks continued, "VM is not a diagnosis on its own; it is usually a condition related to other diagnoses. I can easily eliminate some things right now." He scanned through the images that the tech had captured. "The rest of your exam here today is pretty good — no clubbed foot, for example. The only other thing that stands out is the absence of a corpus callosum so far. It should have started forming by now, and I don't see anything there yet."

"So he's missing part of his brain? Isn't that a big deal?" *What about now? Should I panic now? No.*

I recalled a film that was shown in my high school human physiology class. It was about people who didn't have a corpus callosum and how their brains rewired themselves to function next to normally. Maybe this wouldn't be such a big deal.

"It's hard to tell at this point. I wouldn't say that it's missing yet. We'll keep watch. If it continues to not show up, then, yes, that's a big deal. It's called ACC – absence of corpus callosum – and it does get associated with VM. We'd also want to be aware of its *full* development. ACC can be partial, so we'll want to note its continued development over the next few weeks.

He continued, "From here we'll suggest more testing to see if we can eliminate other possibilities, keep watch on the VM and corpus callosum, and see if we can identify a clearer prognosis. I'll see you again in a week, but in the meantime, Natalie will help you through the next steps."

Immediately Dr. Brooks introduced us to a genetic counselor, with whom we sat down. She was having a busy day — we were the third VM case this week, and actually one of them was down the hall right at that moment. "Oh, so this is kinda common?"

"No, not really. It occurs in 1% of pregnancies nationally. Here, maybe less than ten a year, but they tend to come in clusters together." *Less than ten.* Natalie walked us through our next steps.

"Our goal is to get you as much information as we can. The deadline for late term termination in Hawai'i is 24 weeks, and if you need more time, in California it's 26. So we'll need to get your appointments quickly if that is something you might consider."

Wow, okay, so we're thinking about that now, are we? Okay.

"To be clear, the deadline is 24 weeks and 0 days, so one day later is too late. Let's look at the calendar so we know what our timeline is." She opened my file and a calendar. "So today you are 19 weeks and 6 days. You'll be 24 weeks and 0 days on Sunday, February 21, but we should look at that Friday, the 19th since you'd want services to be available."

I notice how you're talking, Natalie. You said "services," but I know what you mean.

"Of course California would give you two more weeks, if you needed more time. You have some time to gather information and decide." *Decide?* The room spun.

Natalie scheduled our next ultrasound with Dr. Brooks, ordered an MRI, set up an amniotic fluid test and a fetal EEG both at their office, set up an appointment with a pediatric neurologist, referred me back to my OB for special blood work, and gave us a stack of genetic history paperwork to help us recall any brain disorders in our family histories. I worried out-loud that the stress of all of this news can't be good for me either; so, she also gave us a referral to a psychologist in the hospital.

I would be at the hospital at least three times a week for several weeks. Each test seemed to lead to more tests, follow-ups, and second opinions. Thank goodness my faculty job had some schedule flexibility — at least in the short-term.

Dan and I left the hospital dumbstruck. Dan was clearly shaken, tense in his muscles, and moist from stress-sweat. We had planned to eat lunch out before picking up Peyton from daycare and heading to the airport for our Maui adventure. Good thing, because we had to get our thoughts together and talk through this. *What the hell just happened?* We went to an udon noodle place that hit the spot — comfort food for our time of deep need.

Dan was still reeling, "For about ten minutes in there, I was elated to be having a boy. For ten minutes I got to feel what that's like. Now, this. We might not ever meet him. How did you know it was coming?"

"I didn't. That tech was so noticeably different from our first one, though. She wasn't chatting with us at all. Maybe that tipped me off."

We decided that we hadn't received clearly bad news, but it was likely to head in that direction.

"How are we going to do this Maui trip?"

"How are we going to tell people this? They are expecting to hear the gender news."

We decided that telling people the truth would leave us open to their judgement if we chose to terminate. We'd be vague. We'd say, "It isn't going well." If we did choose to terminate, we'd say we "lost the baby," implying miscarriage. But, we could tell our family. And these friends waiting for us in Maui, they were good friends. We could tell them the whole story — just what we needed.

We called and told our families the news of Liko's situation. We picked up our 18-month-old and headed to the airport. She was, of course, oblivious to our news and was her happy-go-lucky self. We allowed ourselves to get taken in by her mood. Once we arrived in Maui, we did tell our friends, and they were more supportive than we could have imagined. We decided we were in Maui, for goodness sake, and we were going to have a great time. We did. For the most part.

While our days were packed with sun, beach, pool, friends, and kid fun, our nights were just plain sad. Our toddler's bed time was early, and since we couldn't leave her unattended in the hotel room, one or both of us would lie in bed in the room with her crib near us. Lying in the quiet dark for hours of wakefulness, careful not to wake our child, our sad thoughts and fears caught up to us. I'd cry while Dan held me. Once Peyton was asleep, Dan and I could share our worst fears and concerns.

Once Dan was asleep, and I still couldn't, I reached out to my friend Eliza via emails.

Chapter 14

Eliza

E liza and I had known each other since elementary school. We drifted apart after fourth grade when her family moved, then we reconnected via social media just within the last few years. Upon reconnecting, I learned that we had grown up quite differently. Eliza had grown up in a type of evangelical Christian home, where mine was more mainline Protestant. As an adult, where I leaned left politically, she leaned right. And yet we had some core similarities — we both had been White girls raised in central Virginia, educated by the same teachers, and loved by similar neighbors and childhood friends. Fundamentally, we were quite similar. I valued her perspective on many contentious issues; she challenged and pushed me in very kind, patient, and smart ways that I valued. I considered her my long-distance conservative consult. I was desperate to get her perspective on the news about our son.

Saturday, January 23, 2010, 12:12 am HST Email to Eliza
Oh Eliza, I can't sleep. Mainly because I can't stop crying. We found out yesterday that we're having a boy....who will most likely have some mental disabilities. To what level, we don't know. I have an amnio on Monday, and an MRI soon thereafter. My guess right now, based on the info we know and the little research we've done so far, is that the

brain is small and that the mass that connects the left and right hemispheres (corpus callosum) is missing. Sigh. Sorry to unload and dump, but there it is. I'm having thoughts that I'm not proud of, and scary thoughts. Dan is being such a great husband. I hope all is well.

Saturday, January 23, 2010, 3:30 am HST Email from Eliza
You didn't unload or dump, Kelly, not at all! I'm so thankful you shared with me. I am so so sorry. I hope with all my heart that this will prove not to be a severe problem for him – sweet little boy. I don't think you should be ashamed of thoughts you're having. . . that's so normal, hon. I'm certain I would be thinking and feeling everything you are. I will be praying for you through this. My heart aches for you, truly. Even the fear alone, before getting all of the facts, is so overwhelming I am sure. I'm glad Dan is being so wonderful. Thank goodness for good hubbies, huh?

Other friends waited to hear the news of our baby's sex. They reminded us via social media that they were waiting. I posted one sentence, "It's a boy!" and received over 100 likes and various congratulatory comments. People were thrilled for us. Some knew of our desire for "one of each" and they were especially happy for us. A few comments were from a group of friends that all had daughters, us included. One of them commented, "Well, pigs DO fly!" I delighted in our friends' pleasure and giddiness. But, it was also difficult to hold onto. Only we knew at the time of the strong possibility that we would disappoint them with sad news in just a few weeks' time. God, I hoped not.

Saturday, January 23, 2010, 11:46 am HST Email from Eliza

Hi, Kelly. You've been on my mind all day. How are you doing? I just went to your wall and saw all of the happy comments on your news. I was thinking about how each of those comments would maybe feel right now, from your perspective — yes, you have joy over a little boy, but sadness over the struggles you fear he may have. Do you want to talk about the scary thoughts you mentioned? I won't judge! Honest! I care about you and want to be here if that would help.

Saturday, January 23, 2010, 12:33 pm HST Email to Eliza

Last night I couldn't stop crying and surfing the internet. So I got to a point where my mind was racing with possibilities. I caused this defect. One cause of ACC (the absence of the corpus callosum) is fetal injury. And contrary to my first pregnancy, this time I ran (and a lot) throughout the first several weeks until I started to "bleed." Doc told me to stop exercising, and the bleeding stopped. So I'm convinced that's when it happened. I thought I never should have run in the first place.

I've thought about our reasons for having a second child, so they'll have each other throughout life, but I think this child may be a burden on Peyton as she gets older. The doctor mentioned termination as an eventual option. And I honestly don't know what it would take for me to seriously consider that. I think about it and cry. What would be worse, living with THAT guilt? Or sacrificing my life and maybe Peyton's to some extent to a very needy child? And I actually don't know! I think about the possibility of

this child feeling a lot like a
pet...developing independence to a point
but then truly NEEDing me forever to
survive. This isn't the son we dreamed of.
College? Contributing to society?
Developing intellectual interests?
Changing the world in some small but
helpful way? None are likely. Then I fear
having so many bad messages in my head,
that I'LL be the one keeping him from
being all he can be. These are my horrible
thoughts, ones I'd likely ever share with
only Dan, my mom, and a counselor. I have
good thoughts too. Seeing him. Him being
beautiful and snuggly. Him being a mama's
boy forever with no need to outgrow it
("MY son"). Dan dreams about us being
disability rights advocates. And I still
think, probably unrealistically, that he
could be fine (I mean he's missing parts
of his brain, how could he possibly be
fine!?).

*Saturday, January 23, 2010, 2:39 pm HST Email from
Eliza*
        I just want you to know that I can
truly understand every feeling you have
expressed here. That sounds like a
perfectly normal, and healthy response.
You're thinking through the possibilities,
and your options in this situation and
processing what all of those possibilities
and choices could mean for you. That's
exactly where I would be. . . I'm sure of
it! It sounds like you are doing a good
job thinking all of this through. I'm glad
you have such a sweet hubby to hold your
hand through this. . . I absolutely love
his dream of being an advocate for
disability rights. He's a good one, Kelly!
Whatever the next months and years hold,
you'll get through it together.

I was thinking about what you said about your hopes for this child, and I completely get that, and it would be my first thought, too. Still, like you said, you have a hope of him "changing the world in some small but helpful way." Kelly, I don't believe that this is going to prevent him from doing that! I'm guessing he will contribute in ways you can't even imagine right now. I think sometimes the greatest joys and blessings in this life come from the people we would least expect, in the ways we would never think possible, and, yes, sometimes in ways we would have never chosen.

Kelly, I just can't fathom a possibility for this child where he will not be given every opportunity to thrive and to impact the world in his own beautiful way. He will have smart, compassionate, non-judgmental parents who will pull out all the stops to allow him every means necessary for his success (true success).

I truly hope you aren't blaming yourself for this!! That's not fair to you! You stopped running when your doc said to — that's what matters. Oh man, I feel like I'm going on and on. At times like this I'm unsure if I'm helping or hurting. . . Please know I care!!! So much! I'm here, hon.

Back at home in Honolulu while I was visibly pregnant, in large part, I was afraid to allow myself to enjoy it. Honestly, I had no idea if I'd be having a baby or not. Strangers made kind, encouraging comments and asked well-intentioned questions. My responses were short and vague, and I tried to end the conversation quickly. If they continued to press, I'd say, "Honestly, it isn't going well, and I'd rather not talk about it." The approaching tears in my eyes were effective signals I could not go any further with the conversation.

Dr. Brooks had mentioned to us that the prognosis for our boy with ventriculomegaly was a mystery, largely because so few cases are brought to term. Most parents-to-be of severe VM babies terminate the pregnancy. We did a little digging in the medical journals and found the largest study of VM pregnancies. In the last twenty years of the data for this study, only eleven severe VMs had been brought to full term (prior to that about 50% were terminated electively, and the other half miscarried or were stillborn). Of the eleven, six died within a month of being born. Of the remaining five, four had a disability of some sort, one was developmentally typical. One. The number of cases researched was too low to make any clear conclusions — or decisions. The prognosis was just unknown. As the weeks progressed Dr. Brooks worked hard to get us more information, but he knew we'd likely need to make a decision without the ability to get any better information than we already had. But each day our time was running out.

Throughout the following weeks, I was easily in the hospital at least three times a week for tests — blood work for infections, amniotic fluid test for chromosomal disorders, MRIs, ultrasounds, genetic counseling, biofeedback counseling, and the fetal EKG for any heart concerns. I wanted Dan to come to as many of these appointments as he could. Sure, I wanted his support, but I also didn't want to be the only one whose job responsibilities would become compromised due to the health concerns of *our* child. Dan came with me for both the amniotic fluid test and the fetal EKG. The needle for the amniotic fluid draw was impressive, easily five inches long. Just the sight of it made Dan sweat. But I took it like a champ. Perhaps the technicians knew our story. They were polite, conversational, and calming, but they didn't talk about our situation or the baby's health. The fetal EKG techs did not take that approach, and it was heartbreaking for us. They were very sweet and encouraging, but it didn't land well. "What a strong healthy heart!?" "Oh, he's so sweet, he's sucking his thumb. I've never seen that before. Do you want to see? I'm going to take a picture." "Do you have any 3-D pictures of him yet? I'll take some for you."

We didn't know what to say. I wanted to see — but only if I knew he would live. "I'm not sure if I want pictures. It could be too hard. He might not make it."

"Well, his heart is the picture of health."

"His heart isn't our main concern. We just wanted to rule out heart problems. It's his brain."

"Oh, I'm sorry, I didn't know."

Yeah, stop being cheery in this place where people come to find out that their baby will die. Suck it. But we both remained pleasant, polite, and just — sad.

Chapter 15

Dr. Tai

I went to the hospital to meet with a pediatric neurologist who would interpret our MRI and ultrasound results. I sat alone in the waiting room. A family consisting of a mother and two daughters walked in. I thought about myself first. *What do they think of me? Do they wonder why I'm sitting in a pediatrician's office without a kid? Maybe they think I'm a medical sales rep? Can they see my slight baby bump?* I wanted to speak up and say to them, *I'm here to see this neurologist about my unborn baby. He's not even born yet, and I'm here. Please feel sorry for me. I do.* But I didn't.

I looked more closely at the family. One child was about eight and trying to read a chapter book. "Mom, what does M-a-c-k-e-n-z-i-e spell?"

"MacKenzie."

"Oh, I thought it was like, mac-a-zine, and that's a weird name."

"Yeah, that would be a weird name."

The other daughter looked to be about 16, and she played with a strand of plastic Mardi Gras beads. At first she massaged them in her hands quietly, then stretched them out to a wide oval. Eventually, she started to shake the beads in the air while moaning in excitement. The mother would shush her and the girl would comply. This continued – play quietly, get excited, shush, quiet – such that the mother's instruction was always followed, but never remembered for long. The mom was visibly annoyed. The girl never spoke. She'd just moan and shake the beads.

So, they are here for her. This girl is the patient.

I recalled my own child's fascination with strands of toy beads when she was ten months old. She'd swing and shake them, put them in her mouth, put them on, take them off, put them on me, take them off. I remembered because it was one of the few activities that could capture her attention for more than ten minutes. And Peyton started speaking at eleven months. *So, this must be a delay. This 16-ish year old girl appears to have the development of a very young child. I'm starting to get it.*

I looked at the mother closely. She looked tired, worn, and even defeated. *Hey Mom. I see you. I am you in a few years' time. Look at my belly. What would you do if you were in my position?*

I was called in to meet with Dr. Tai before the other family. I felt awkward walking in with no child with me. I wasn't sure if I should push out my belly from behind my cardigan or hold it in, so I made no particular effort either way. My arms became heavy as I entered. Dr. Tai reviewed my MRI images and helped us to finally settle on a diagnosis.

"As you know VM is not a diagnosis, it's a symptom. What I think we're looking at here is a case of aqueductal stenosis, or AS. There's probably a block in his spinal fluid circulatory system." He pointed at the MRI image, "I see not only enlarged lateral ventricles," then he pointed to the ultrasound image, "but also the third ventricle is slightly enlarged. Measurements for the ventricles will ebb and flow, so as you continue to get measurements on his ventricles, with AS, lower readings don't mean as much. They could go back up in a few days."

I nodded.

"I have a few patients with AS."

"What is their life like? What kind of disabilities do they have?"

"Well, all of them need to have a shunt to bypass the blockage and keep the spinal fluid circulating."

"What's a shunt? How does it work?"

"It's a tube that is placed on the head, it sits outside of the body, and it allows the fluid to be drained from the ventricles. To be blunt, I drill a hole through the skull and the tube runs down into the ventricles; then the other end is led down to the belly for draining, and it's absorbed there. The best-case scenario is that one shunt can last for years. They'll need to get replaced from time to time mostly because the child outgrows it, but sometimes there are complications that need to be addressed. Some patients have them replaced more than others."

"So this is a surgery each time?"

"Yes."

"A brain surgery?"

"Well, yes."

"And otherwise they are typical?"

"Some, but most have some sort of accompanying mental or physical disability."

"Like what?"

"Oh, all over the place — learning disabilities, developmental delays, cerebral palsy, just to name few."

Dan and I later hit the medical journals and discovered that AS is a leading cause for hydrocephalus, and I had heard of that — "water on the brain" that left kids with very large heads and small brains. I supposed that's why the shunt would help. The prognosis for AS was scary to see — 40% mortality rate, 10% typical development, 50% wide range of disabilities. *Ugh.*

I had visions of taking my child in for countless surgeries — calming his nerves before each one, all the while aware of my own. I envisioned the disabled adults that Shannon worked with years before. The ones who lived in a home where she fed, bathed, and diapered some of them. Where she took them out for occasional field trips as onlookers jeered. The place where she was the most qualified staff member with her almost college degree, where some other staff members abused the residents. The home where most families visited on occasion, but some never visited. Would that be our son? Would we raise him and grow tired of the demands, and pay someone to take him off of our hands? I didn't want to make this decision based on the cute and appropriate dependence of a child. I wanted to consider what his quality of life would be over his entire life. And ours. And Peyton's.

The normal amnio, EKG, and blood tests results were encouraging. Through two weeks of repeated imaging tests we could see that Liko's ventricle sizes continued to be large, but with slightly lower measurements (13mm), now into the moderate category. And the corpus callosum *was* beginning to develop, but very slowly. We wanted to believe these were all good bits of news, but Dr. Brooks and Dr. Tai continued to remain cautious, noting that AS will fluctuate. And they also noted the third ventricle, under the lateral ventricles, was unusually large.

Due to my experience at Pearl Harbor, none of this felt personal any longer. No part of me wondered if Liko was doomed to die because I was his mom and that's just what happens "to me." At this point I trusted that life just happens and what was happening to our son and us was just life – our life, but life just the same.

I had adopted Miriam's perspective that "this isn't about me," and I was still learning to avoid projecting my own backstory and baggage onto the similar yet unrelated events before me. Just as Nick's death from cancer was similar yet unrelated to Miriam's cancer recurrence, my past repeated experiences with death were similar yet unrelated to my own son's survival story. From my lessons with Rebecca's death, I saw that I had a choice to either resist or accept our news about Liko as is. I saw how resistance was an attractive path; it came with a hopeful, yet false, sense of control that aimed to avoid uncomfortable emotions. Acceptance would mean admitting a loss of control and experiencing overwhelming agony. Sometimes, though, we underestimate the breadth of our control; we give into misery too decisively. I noticed a paradox — that often it is healthy to have a sense of control over your life; and also it is unhealthy to believe you have control when you do not. Wisdom is knowing the difference…the essence of the serenity prayer. The difference is knowing that, with mindful practice, we *do* have control over our own perceptions, thoughts, experiences, and boundaries; but we do *not* have control over life's circumstances or other people. We can shift to accept both our circumstances and the people around us.

I began to see that my past of viewing life events through a self-centering narrative had effectively led me to believe I could control life events and, consequently, that belief put me in a position to resist the way things were. I had feared becoming like

Rebecca, but I already was. Now, though, with this news about Liko's health, so far I was choosing to accept it.

I knew big considerations were before us but I felt that the moment to panic had not yet arrived. We soon met someone who would push me much closer to panic.

Chapter 16

Dr. Jansen

O ur genetic counselor, Natalie, referred us to Dr. Galen Jansen, a psychologist on the staff at the hospital who helped people deal with making difficult health decisions. Our meeting with Dr. Jansen was intended to help us make a decision for our son. Jansen also skillfully talked us through our sadness and stress, and our relationship. Jansen was pale and tall, with salt and pepper hair with more salt than pepper in his trim beard. He reminded me of my high school history teacher, trustworthy and relatable. His office was quite small, with no windows, only a chair for him and a couch for Dan and me.

For decision-making, he encouraged us to explore the feelings associated with each decision. He wanted us to "try on" the worst-case scenario for both decisions. He made it clear that there was no middle-ground or compromise; we'd either choose to terminate or not. So we needed to go there and talk through the worst feeling associated with each decision.

I worried that either way we decided might jeopardize our marriage. Dan would say, "It's your body, your choice, and I'll just support you." As kind as I'm sure that sounded in his head, it sucked ass. "Don't put this horrible decision on me because I'm carrying the baby. I've got enough burden here. Don't pile on more shit on top of that. Don't leave me here alone in this fucked up situation while you get to kick back and 'support me.' Fuck that. Fuck your support. I don't want your support. I want you right here making this decision. I want you in the middle of this, feeling just as responsible and just as emotional as I do. I want you checked in. You don't get to check-out, Asshole. Not an option." Maybe I didn't say it exactly that way, but that's certainly how I felt.

He understood, but rather than accept that he needed to shift his perspective and move forward, he back-pedaled and tried to rationalize why what he said was still in line with what he thought I'd asked for. It wasn't. I thought, *just shut up and shift. You will eventually, so do it now rather than continuing to defend your stupid comment and inciting my anger. Stop talking.*

Fortunately, Dr. Galen was there for the rescue. "It really isn't in your own best interest or your relationship to leave the decision to Kelly. You could be setting yourself up for resentment, for either decision. You really need to think deeply about what you want and articulate that and have that input be part of the decision-making. If you don't bother to name your concerns now, it can only backfire later. Kelly carrying the baby has little relevance to the decision. This child is both of yours."

And that was that. Dan was invested in the decision.

First we talked through the worst-case scenario with termination.

"How much have you two been told about late-term terminations?"

"Well, nothing actually. I did find out that my OBGYN can do it, but I have no idea how it would go. I assumed they'd just reach in and get it."

"Later term options are limited. You'd actually be induced, and sign a do-not-resuscitate order, a DNR, beforehand."

Hot tears instantly streamed down my face, dripping into my cupped hands in my lap. Since I'd already given birth once, I knew exactly what this meant. "I'd go into labor?"

"Yes."

"And feel contractions?!"

"Yes, and you'd need to push. That can be very difficult to do."

"No kidding. That sucks. That's the worst. People do this?"

"Yes."

Dan just sat there and watched me.

"And then the baby would be born alive? And we'd have to watch it die? Just sit there and watch it die?"

"Well, often at that age the fetus is very calm, and not really stirring or being conscious yet. Any movement you'd see would be reflexes, not consciousness. This won't be a crying healthy baby. It'll be an extremely underdeveloped fetus that's not viable."

"I couldn't stand seeing it. It would be an image that would haunt me forever. I wouldn't want to see it." More tears fell, enlarging the wet spot on my shirt.

"Your doctor can honor your wish, but many parents in this situation find that they have a much better chance at emotional healing if they can see the fetus and even say their goodbyes. The fetus gets wrapped in a blanket and held by the parents. No machinery is hooked up, so there's no real knowledge of when the fetus passes. It's all very peaceful and loving. And, yes, sad. You'd feel better knowing that your son left this world being held and loved by his parents. Some even take pictures together. We have an annual birthday party at the hospital for these families who mourn the loss of a fetus or infant. Many have pictures." I cried even harder as he spoke.

"I could see that being helpful to me, too." My tears choked the clarity of my soft voice. "It has been easier for me to experience closure after death when I've been able to see a body." And I wiped my face with my bare hand.

My eyes widened and my voice became more clear. "I can't go through that, then hop on a plane back to Hawai'i from California. Hell, the trip out there would be torture. If we do that, it would have to be here in Honolulu. So our deadline is 24 weeks firm."

Dan instantly agreed, "Right that would be a horrible trip both ways."

"That sounds like a good decision for both of you."

"That's probably the only decision I feel comfortable making."

Jansen kept us thinking, "Now, consider what you might want to do with the remains."

"Oh really?! Really? I have to think about the remains too?" I opened my eyes wider so I could see him past the tears pooling in my eye.

"Of course."

"God, this keeps getting worse," a giant tear splashed down my shirt.

"For some, this can be empowering with regard to shaping how you'd want to remember your son."

My voice cleared, "I wouldn't want to bury him here, because we may not stay in Hawai'i. I'm only tenure track, my professional fate is not in my hands. If we left, he'd be alone here. So, I guess that means cremation. But I don't think I'd want to carry him around with me. There just doesn't seem to be any good place to keep him."

"There's a lot to consider, but you do have time for those decisions. Focus on your feelings now. Tell me how this scenario feels."

"It feels like deep emotional trauma. It feels like I'll never get over this. Scarred for life. Like I may not even be able to get through it as it happens. Like I'll die from heartbreak before the fetus is even born. I can see me changing my mind on the spot, 'no, don't give me that Pitocin shot, I can't do this, even if I know I should.' Or worse, changing my mind after the shot. I could see my life forever falling apart from the emotional trauma of having experienced that.

"When I was a young adult, I was late on my period for two weeks, and I was convinced I was pregnant but afraid to find out. It turned out I was just late, probably exacerbated by my stress of the recent devastating break-up with a boy. I wasn't even pregnant, and I think about that kid occasionally. *How old would he be now?* I just can't begin to imagine what it would be like to lose this real boy to my own decision. I think I'd feel better about him being still-born than a termination.

"I could see this event consuming the rest of my days. Meeting people his age and wondering what he'd look like. What he'd be good at? Who would he have become? The forever unknown. If this is the route we go, it would be a defining moment in my life, and I'd hope to become strong and gain character from it. But I'm certain I would struggle to do so.

"And I'm not a big secret person. But I'd have to be on this one. I don't want to be openly honest about what happened, because I don't want to be at the mercy of people's judgements. No thank you. But somehow I'd have to explain to people how all of a sudden, I'm not pregnant anymore, and there's no baby. I'd just want to say vaguely, 'he didn't make it.' I'm already telling people 'it's not going well,' getting them primed for the possibility of something tragic happening. They already know not to engage me in pregnancy small talk."

"Dan, how are you feeling?"

"Pretty lousy. I'd obviously be right there in the room when it happened, and I would be sad, of course. But, I'd be beside myself watching Kelly give birth. Utterly helpless. To see her go through that would definitely affect me."

"Let's try on the other decision. What would be the worst-case scenario?"

"Not much better, honestly. For me the worst isn't him having a disability at all. It's specifically a severe and profound disability, which for this boy is a possibility, though we don't know how likely."

"So, give me a tour of that life."

"I can't tell you how unprepared I was for how dependent my daughter was as a newborn. I knew it in my head, but to live it represented a new level of awareness for me. So much utter dependence stifled my own liberties. I couldn't eat, sleep, or use the restroom when I wanted. Her needs were constant. Without me serving her, she'd starve, dehydrate, and sit in her own filth. My dad had the best insight to share with me as a new parent, 'they only get more and more independent every day.' That comment saved me. I could see that she'd hold her own bottle and that was a milestone. Then she'd eat solid foods, learn to use the potty, and dress herself. I know one day she'll click her own seatbelt buckle. With each milestone, I could see that I would get my own liberties back. One day, I'll be able to do a project in my house while my daughter is awake. I could get something, anything, else done and develop my own interests.

"But with a severely and profoundly disabled kid, that would go away. I would go away. I'd be spoon-feeding and diaper changing my 18-year-old while I wondered who would

take care of him after I died. Not a few months straight of
dependence on one particular task, but the rest of my lifetime,
with no end in sight. And I'd certainly die younger, from the
heartbreak of having to give up all hope of having interests,
skills, and an identity of my own. I didn't get a PhD to keep my
professional contributions to myself. I wanted to matter to my
profession. I wanted my brain to matter. I wanted to be
somebody. Being someone's servant for life was not my
ambition, even my own son, whom I know I would adore."
　　Jansen watched Dan, "What about you, Dan?"
　　"I see it differently. I see roses and rainbows and rigging
up wheelchair ramps, being in a new parent circle, and Special
Olympics. I don't see my wife disappearing because honestly I
never felt that her professional contribution would be valuable
anyway. I am the man and can't see how women's lives are more
affected than mine. My privilege is rosy and smells good."
　　No, that's not what he said; but it is what I heard.
　　I'm aware that to some my concerns might sound selfish,
but when the question of my own humanity and liberty is on the
line, then I think I'm allowed to matter. Folks who want to judge
me for that can bug off.
　　In either scenario I feared losing my humanity, of being
deeply affected. I liked myself in that moment. I felt I was either
going to die from heartache from losing my son or die from
heartache from losing myself.

　　Liko's health, and life, felt deeply out of my control. I was
open to any strategy that might help our situation that would also
have no risk of making things worse. I took daily omega-3 fatty
acid tablets for brain health after being assured by Dr. Brooks
that there would be no risk. I decided to participate in pregnancy
yoga again with an optimistic outlook. Our psychologist
encouraged us to use biofeedback techniques. A relaxed body is
in a better position to heal than a stressed body, and I believed
that. Dr. Jansen gave me several mindfulness stress reduction
audio recordings to listen to at bedtime, which I did every night.
Dan told me about a triathlete he read about who had a major
injury. The athlete would close his eyes before sleeping and

imagine tiny working men entering his body and working on reconstructing his body from the inside out throughout the night — healing through visualization. And it worked. So we closed our eyes and pictured Liko's incredibly tiny head in our hands. In my mind's eye, he had dark brown hair. I held his tiny head in my right hand like an orange in the palm of my hand. I kissed his brown hair at the spot where my thumb and forefinger meet to make the L-shape. My imaginary-self closed her eyes and pictured the insides of Liko's brain. *Shrink the ventricles, condense, and heal.*

I hoped that this visualization wasn't enabling our susceptibility to denial given our circumstances.

I told a work friend about our healing strategies, "It's not important to me if these things are proven to work or not. I just need to feel like I'm doing something. Even if these methods were placebos, they were something to do."

She told me of an energy healer she had used in the past. I was curious. "What does she do?"

"Oh she reads your chakras, hovers her hands above your body, and 'sends light' to heal you."

"Does she ever touch your body?"

"Nope."

"Does she need for you to believe in it for it to work?"

"Nope."

"Sounds exactly like something I would be open to." So I took her recommendation and called Carol.

Carol met me at our home when I was alone. She charged by the hour, and I thought that's all we'd need. I started by telling her the whole story. She was very interested. She was an RN and had had a long career working in hospitals. Her current career, for her, was about exploring alternative healing, which she found deeply compelling. She was such a great listener. I didn't care how long our talking went on, I needed it. It was valuable. Most of our time together was talk therapy. I asked her about energy healing.

"Is it a religion?"

"Not really. No supernatural deities."

"But, you see things I don't see — chakras, auras."

"Yes, well, it's a matter of training. You could see them too with guidance and practice. And maybe you have, but didn't know what you saw."

"And what is this light that heals? Where is that?"

"Some people interpret it as a being or God, but that's not my perspective. It's a powerful light in our universe, and it can be summoned and sent to specific places. I use my hands to draw and focus the light."

"Do I have to believe in it for it to work?"

She cracked a smile. "Oh, no, not at all. It's there whether you believe in it or not. I have clients who joke with me through our meetings. Total doubters. But they know they feel better, so they keep up the meetings."

She explained everything she did, as she read my aura and chakras. We each have six chakras that dot the center line of our body. Each chakra is a colored circle light and represents a certain part of life. If the chakra has a healthy glow, that part of life is good. If it's dim or gone, that part of your life is injured or blocked. We talked about each of these areas of my life, as she interpreted the manifestation of each of my chakras. We started down and went up, and skipped to only key chakras of interest. I told her of my dead exes, and I fantasized that they hung out with me. She said I was surrounded by old love.

As she concluded the tour of my chakras, she paused and smiled at me, "So the top of your head is the spirituality chakra. What do you think yours looks like?"

"I guess it depends on how you define spiritual. I don't subscribe to any religious beliefs. I actively avoid it. Actually, lately, I've been saying I'm atheist. So, it would probably be dim."

"Well, your spirituality chakra is your most healthy one."

"Really?"

"Oh, yeah, nice purple glow."

"So what does that mean?"

"Well, it doesn't reflect religious belief in particular, but rather a higher sense of purpose. Some get that from religion, but many don't. It reflects self-awareness and a higher consciousness…a seeking of purpose in all things."

Seeking of purpose? Yes, that's what I do. I'll take it.

Next, it was time for her to read Liko's chakras and send him some light. She saw the alignment of his chakras and could already tell his orientation in my belly without even touching me. "His head is over here, and his back is along the left. He's not tight at all; he has room in there for getting comfortable."

Next, she instructed me to stand comfortably but keep silent. Carol focused hard. She swayed her arms in fluid motions. She put her hands very close to me, but never touched. Her hands were strong and soft. She moved from my front to side to back, focusing deeply with her hands, and sweeping motions. After circling me once, she came to my belly and focused there hard. I could feel heat coming from her hands. She would motion her hands toward the sunlight in the room, then press her flat palms toward my belly without touching. She did this several times.

"How is he? Is he going to make it? Could you fix it?"

"I did everything I can do. I certainly sent a lot of light there. But it's between him and the light if that will be enough. His chakras tell the same story that you do. There's definitely a health concern that his body feels…in his head. And there's a lot of love there, too. You two have an old connection."

I melted. "I've wondered if one of my exes or dead friends would come back to me through my children."

"Oh, this is a deeper and older love. You two have been together for several lives, and always have cared for each other deeply."

"Oh, so this energy healing view of life includes reincarnations?"

"Yes, more or less. The universe is swimming in beings, and every now and then one will become born to experience human life, and they can do this multiple times. They learn deep lessons with each human lifetime that they take with them to their next life, without their human-self really knowing where the lesson came from. As humans our consciousness is limited to this life, but our wisdom is not. You and your boy are both old. If he doesn't make it this go around, you'll see him again."

Well, that made me cry, and feel relieved, too. *It's okay that I don't have control. It's okay, if the absolute worst happens.*

The worst is that I don't get to know him this go around, but I already do know him in the deep recesses of my own wisdom. I have him in my life already. The tears were because I really wanted to know him during this lifetime of mine. It would be a long wait by human standards to see him again. And I already knew I missed him.

I leaned into Carol's explanations and beliefs. I didn't bother myself with trying to decide if they were true; I believed that no one could know the truth. But Carol's explanations gave me feelings of relief and peace, regardless of how this would unfold. If it turned out that her beliefs hold truth, then I would be grateful that she assisted us. Either way, I was grateful and desperate for any strategy that might work.

Our mothers told us of their prayers, including sharing their prayers with others. Dan's mother had a group of five Prayer Warriors, who in turn had Prayer Partners. A whole posse of praying folk were out there, not just thinking of us, but praying for us. I hadn't prayed in years, and didn't bother this time. I had come to believe it was all bunk. As we had each image or test, we'd tell our family what we'd hoped for, and they'd pass it on to the Prayer Warriors. We hoped for clear blood work and amnio tests, and we got it. We asked for a clear fetal EKG test, and we got it. We asked for lower VM measurements, and we got it. We asked to spot some development of the corpus callosum, and we got it. Perhaps the prayers worked. Perhaps.

Though we got good news, we also got bad. Monday of Week 22, February 8, we visited with Dr. Jansen again to continue to talk through our decisions. He shared with us news that he had heard from Dr. Brooks: our son's prognosis had been estimated at 80-90% chance of a mental disability with a wide range of severity possible.

"Well that's helpful to know. It hadn't been put into terms of numbers yet, and that's something clearer. Still painfully vague, but something we can start to work with."

"When I visited with him and his team, well, you should know, folks here are delighted to work with you. You've been such a pleasure for everyone. Several other families have received similar news over the course of the last few weeks, and some have taken it out on the fetal diagnostics staff. Dr. Brooks and Natalie have been yelled at a few times this week."

"Oh no." Dan sounded genuinely concerned. "It's not their fault."

"Right, well, it's also a very normal reaction to that kind of news. It feels so devastating and powerless as you know. And the messenger is an easy target."

I wanted to prepare our family for a possible future termination decision. I feared them focusing too much on the good news. I wanted them to be able to support our termination decision if one was made. I gave them every grave disturbing bit of news we had. I made no effort to spare them those details, because it would be those details that would allow them to support us through a termination choice.

My mom called. She struggled to hear me sound conflicted, "Can you view a termination as disease prevention? I mean, aren't you pro-choice? Why is this decision hard?"

"Because this is our boy, Mom. We want *this* boy, if we can have him."

"I understand that, but it's not going well."

"Yeah, but he's real. A real kid inside me. My own kid, not a political statement. Yes, I'm pro-choice, but that doesn't mean the choice is easy."

"I'm so sorry, honey. This is very hard."

Thanks, Mom. Yes it is hard.

The news we hoped for wasn't necessarily just good news. Even clear bad news would be helpful. But with each subsequent test, we saw improved ventricle measurements, and no other accompanying complications. Making a decision based on "middle" information was overwhelming. Various doctors warned us against focusing too much on the improved measurements, these things can get better and then worse. Also the severe measurements were real and some undetermined damage had happened.

Dr. Brooks was thrilled to connect us to "the best in the state," Dr. Tanaka, for a second opinion. We saw him on the Wednesday of week 22, nine days until our deadline. For this appointment, we had our wish list that I'm sure had been conveyed to our family's Prayer Warriors.

During the exam, Dr. Tanaka was quiet for quite a while, not making eye contact and intensely focused on my belly and the images on the ultrasound. He excused himself and left the room. He returned with three thick medical textbooks, each filled with sample ultrasound images and text descriptions. He flipped pages one direction, then the other.

I grew impatient, "So what do you see?"

"Well, I want to compare what I see to…" and he trailed off. "This isn't it. It's not in any of these. Excuse me." And he left again.

Dan said, "Uh-oh, is this worse? Something he's never seen before? Jeez, can we catch a break?"

"He's supposed to be the best in the state, how is this something he hasn't seen before?"

He returned. "Yes, this is the one." He held up a thick book. "This one has the image I'm looking for." And he showed us the pages as he flipped through a middle section, and he stopped. "Here," and he pointed.

"What are we looking at?"

"I don't look at the third ventricle very often. Usually the lateral ventricles tell us all we need to know. So I needed a reminder of what it should look like. There aren't standard measurements for the third ventricle, so we're looking at shape and using judgements." He closed the book and looked directly into our eyes for the first time. "Ehh…it doesn't look that bad to me." He shrugged.

"What? How?" I was doubtful. I looked at Dan. He gleamed. *Shit.*

"Well, the third ventricle looks normal to me. I know there was concern about a block there, but I don't see it."

"What about nonclassical aqueductal stenosis? That wouldn't involve the third ventricle."

"Yeah, that's possible." And he shrugged.

"And what about the laterals?"

"It's 12 millimeters now, the low end of moderate. Again, doesn't look that bad to me."

"We've been told not to get our hopes up over lower lateral ventricle measurements. That they can ebb and flow with aqueductal stenosis."

"Yes. That's possible." He shrugged again.

"What about the corpus callosum?"

"Right. Let's look at that." And he picked up the wand again. *He didn't look yet?* "So it would be here…I don't see it… Oh, I see it here, but I don't see the whole thing. Wait let me try…" He switched angles. "Ri-ight here? No. No, I don't quite see it all. Watch with me." And he pointed at the screen with one hand while he moved the wand with the other. "See it's here, and I follow it along, and lose it here. I can only see about 1/3 to ½ of it. But should I see it all? Should it be here?" He picked up my file. "You're 22 weeks. And when should we see it all? Um, let me see. Excuse me." He called in his office assistant. "Can you bring in that book with the green spine?"

"Which?" She asked. And he left to find the book.

"Shouldn't he know?" I asked Dan.

"Yeah, I don't know. He makes a good point. We should know when it should be there," Dan said. *Ugh.*

He entered with another thick textbook. "Yeah, see," he pointed in his book, "it should be here in its entirety, but it's not. But honestly, this doesn't really concern me very much. It *has* started."

"We've been told about partial ACC. Could it be possible that its late development could yield a partial formation?"

"Right, yes. That's possible. But, is it likely?"

"Well is it?"

"Not very. I don't see any other symptoms of partial ACC. No lines or higher third ventricle."

"But our whole situation here has been *not very likely*, correct?"

"Yes, true. I wouldn't rule out partial ACC. But, look, in sum, this doesn't look that bad to me. I understand that it used to look worse, but now, it's not. This doesn't even look like aqueductal stenosis to me."

My mind spun. *Why do I think this is bad news? Why doesn't this good news feel good?*

During our walk back to the car, Dan had a spring in his step. "I thought that was a great appointment."

"Yeah?" I held my tongue. I couldn't put words to my feelings.

"Well, don't you think so? He says it doesn't look that bad to him."

"To him."

"Well, he's the best in the state."

"Right, and he had to keep whipping out the textbooks."

"I thought he was thorough."

"Yeah, I could see that."

We got into the car to start our drive back to work. Dan asked, "So what did *you* think?"

"Um, I'm not sure how to put it into words. Not as positive as you."

"Oh, really?"

"Yeah."

"Don't you want good news?"

"I don't want good news for the sake of good news. I want it to be true. I'm not sure I believe him."

"Yeah, I feel that way a little bit, but mostly hopeful. Why is it so hard for you to believe?"

"So here it is. This is it. Tanaka is the only guy telling us good things. *The only one.* The others say, don't get too caught up in lower measurements. This guy's opinion doesn't make the others go away. So now we have mixed opinions to deal with. I want unequivocal information to make a good decision. Honestly? In either direction, I swear. I just want it to be clearly good, or clearly bad. That's what I want. I can't make decisions with this conflicting shit."

"Well, I'm kind of excited." Gut punch.

I instantly cried, "I'm not." If this is the best information we'd get. I would want to terminate, while Dan here would be *kind of excited.* Great.

"You're leaning toward going for it, aren't you?" I asked.

"Well, yeah. I think I am."

"And I'm not. I'm leaning toward termination." Silence in the car. Nothing. *Why won't you respond to me? Are you mad at me? Jesus. I need support. I'm crumbling.* "We're not going to make it as a couple are we? We can't. We can't both make this decision. One of us will be deeply hurt and easily resentful. Either way. Never mind the hurt that the experience alone will bring. We'll struggle to support each other through it, when deep down we'll only think of blame."

"You can make the decision. I'll support you."

"You know that's not what I want to hear."

"What else am I supposed to say?"

"I don't know. I wish my concerns were convincing to you. That you'd want the same thing I do. But you don't. I'm sorry."

"I guess I could say the same."

"Right. You could." *And I guess that means you are saying that, so thanks for that.*

And then we both went back to our offices for the day with this conversation in our heads. That night I sat and wrote a long email to Dr. Brooks explaining our current situation. "We can't help but wonder if you, Dr. Brooks, and Dr. Tanaka are looking at similar images and having different opinions, or if there has been some actual change in a positive direction for the prognosis of our child." I expressed that we had come to appreciate and trust Dr. Brooks's guarded opinion and we sought his input on these new results.

First thing Thursday morning, Dr. Brooks's assistant called us. "Dr. Brooks wanted me to call you. He got your email. He wants you to come in tomorrow at 11:00 am. It's his last appointment before lunch, so he can spend his lunch hour with you, too."

On Friday, with one week until our deadline? "Wow, yes! Yes! That's great. We can do that."

"He wants to do another ultrasound and get a few more opinions and discuss those with you."

"Great! Absolutely."

The next day Dan and I both came in for the appointment with Dr. Brooks.

"What do we hope for today?" Dan asked me.

"Just consistent information. I just want everyone to be on the same page, so we can make a decision based on one opinion and not several conflicting opinions."

"Right. That would be good."

"That's my hope. I trust the openness and honesty of Dr. Brooks. If the opinions we get are still conflicting, I'll yield to him."

Usually, when we had an ultrasound appointment at the hospital, the tech would take measurements, then Dr. Brooks would come in later. Not this time. The tech and Dr. Brooks came in together.

Dr. Brooks seemed chipper, "First, I must say, what a wonderfully written email!"

I beamed. *Oh that's me. I did that. Um, thanks.*

"I *do* respect Dr. Tanaka very much. I absolutely take seriously any observations he makes. Yes, both of your speculations are possible, I could have been interpreting the same images differently, or we could have been looking at different things. First, I want to take a quick look to see what Dr. Tanaka saw."

He prepped the wand, machine, and my belly, and did a quick reading. He showed the tech first, then us; "11 millimeters; that's in the mild range."

"Really?" I said. Chills flashed through my whole body starting at my ankles and leaving through my cheeks. *That's just two millimeters off from normal!*

"Whoa." Dan muttered.

"Really." He looked each of us straight in the eye with a small smile, "This verifies our current understanding. As soon as I saw your email and received Dr. Tanaka's report, I gathered all of your imaging history and packaged it to send to three other prenatal diagnosticians across the nation whom I deeply respect. One is my mentor, unequivocally the best prenatal neurosonographer in the country. I worked with him in Philadephia at Penn. But, I'm not just biased, he really is the best. Anyone would say so." He quickly looked to the floor, realizing that he had practically bragged about himself.

I was stunned. "Okay. Wow, that's amazing! Thank you." *Our case is on the radar of the best guy in the country? Is...is that a good thing? I guess so. I mean, we're going to get good information, then, right? I was honored to receive such outstanding attention for our situation.*

"The others are also top in the field, one at the Children's National Hospital in Washington, DC and another in Minneapolis. I sent each one the images and requested their opinion independent of the others."

"And?"

"Well, all three agreed, again without conferring with each other..."

"Right."

"Their best explanation of the images is that there had been a blockage in the spinal circulatory system around 18 to 19 weeks, like a scab likely caused by an early brain bleed. With time it has dislodged, and it seems to have passed. There's strong evidence that the block will completely clear. The block was temporary, and that's kind of rare."

My jaw dropped. "Wha-?" *The energy healer's light worked. It worked.*

"Our concern now is to question the nature of the earlier brain bleed. If it bled into the ventricle, the blood was likely swept into the system fluid, and it dissipated. If bleeding went *into* the brain, that would be our worst-case scenario at this point. If all remains normal as it's been tracking, my mentor says 80-90% chance of normalcy, and I regard that with the highest respect. Therefore, that's my prognosis for you."

Oh my God. "That's...that's completely the opposite of just earlier this week."

"I know. But, he says to be aware that the severe measurements *were* there. A bleed *did* happen to cause that block. We don't know anything about it. Either that event or the severe measurements that lasted for several weeks afterward can have an impact on development. That's what the 80% chance is for."

"I'll take it. That's not much different from the chances our daughter has."

"Or you or I."

"Yes," air jumped out of my chest as I coughed, laughed, and finally exhaled at the same time. "That's right."

Dan grabbed my hand with two of his. He gently shook it and held it firm in his lap.

I looked him right in the eye, "This is an easy decision."

He beamed and grinned his goofy grin showing all his teeth, "It is." I loved him. "We're having a boy," he said.

"Well," Dr. Brooks continued, "I want to point out that this is the unified speculation. That this interpretation makes sense of every image we see, including today, as one whole story. To verify this story, though, and to take a look at the nature of the earlier brain bleed, I'd like to see one more fetal MRI. Let's schedule that as soon as we can. When is your deadline?"

"A week from today." But I was pretty certain that it didn't matter now.

"We can make that work. I'll be sure of it." He spoke with the tech for a moment and wrote some notes on his clipboard. "It's such a pleasure to be able to give you two this news. You have been so pleasant to work with. Some people blame the messenger."

"Yeah, we've heard. Sorry that you had to go through that," Dan said.

I joined in, "I can't tell you how appreciative we are of your attention to our situation. Of course this is great news, but that's not what has made working with you so wonderful. We appreciate your dedication to getting us good information, regardless of what it is. You're not responsible for the quality of the news, just your best attempts at correct information. We just want to make a good decision."

"Not everyone understands that," he said while looking at the floor. "I came to work here in Honolulu from New York City, where tolerance for disability was low." I noticed the scar on his lip. "Until recently, most of my experience has been that parents decide to terminate as soon as an issue comes up, which doesn't really require me to find out much more information. But you all wanted to know more, and it was my pleasure to seek it out."

"Well, we struggled with that, too. Just having no idea what we were looking at and what we were willing to live with."

"It's been a pleasure working with you."

You are so kind. I want to know you. I want you to know us. I want you to see this boy grow up. Will you be my friend?

Can we hang out with you at potlucks, lu'aus, and cookouts?
"We'll definitely keep in touch and let you know how it goes."

"Yes, please do. I am interested to know how his development unfolds. Natalie will get you set up for an MRI, and I'll call you with results."

As Dan and I walked out of the hospital, we walked on clouds. I even skipped.

Dan said, "We're having a boy!"

"Probably."

"Why probably?"

"Well, let's see the last round of MRI results, and make the final call then. I don't want to get my hopes up too high in case we get a curve ball from those tests. But, yes, it looks very likely that we're having a boy."

Dan looked at me as if to say, *Really? You're still holding out?*

"Look, the whole adventure has been a roller coaster ride with very low lows, and this could be a very high up. I'm holding out to protect my heart. I'm not a pessimist, Dan; I'm a realist. The roller coaster is real."

"Well, I'm going to feel happy."

"Oh, me too. I'm not sure what they could possibly say next week about the MRI that would turn me back toward a termination decision, but this adventure has taught me that it's possible. I'm just slightly guarded."

I debated how to share this very good news with the family. With the slight possibility that things could still go sideways, I wanted to keep them sympathetic to a possible last-minute termination decision next week.

In our usual hospital, Kapi'olani, the MRI machine was scheduled to be closed on Monday and Tuesday for equipment upgrades and maintenance. Natalie got us into nearby Queen's Hospital in downtown Honolulu instead for an early Monday appointment. The techs there didn't know me. They didn't know my story or why I was there. They didn't seem to notice that I was standing right there in front of them. *Hi, I'm a person. Do you see me here? I've been through some rough days these past few weeks, thanks for asking.* I liked the Kapi'olani staff much better. The rest of Monday and nearly all Tuesday came and went with no news from Dr. Brooks. The clock was ticking. I needed some information. If the news was bad, I'd need to make an appointment for *this* Friday with my OB-GYN. I called Dr. Brooks's office late Tuesday to learn that the Queen's staff hadn't sent over the images yet. They were too large to electronically send, so Dr. Brooks's office was in need of a physical package. I volunteered to be the messenger myself. First thing on Wednesday morning, two days left until my deadline, Brooks's office called ahead to notify the Queen's staff that I was coming. I went to Queen's and waited for the package, then made my way through the Honolulu traffic. Sitting next to me in the car, the answer regarding my future was in that package, but I knew I couldn't read it, so it stayed sealed. And this test seemed like a formality for a result that I already knew. When I arrived at Kapiʻolani by noon, Dr. Brooks wasn't in. He was "off island" and I'd need to wait until the evening. Now, if I seriously thought that I might undergo a termination on Friday, I sure would have not waited for these results to confirm it; I would have made the appointment and canceled if it turned out that I didn't need it. But I had no such appointment, and no concern about a lack of an appointment. I trusted that this news would be good.

At 8:45 pm Dr. Brooks called, "I'm sorry for my late response. I was on Kauaʻi today."

"Thanks for calling into your evening hours. You're a hard-working guy."

"Well, I know this is critical information at a critical time." And he shared with us the best news we could imagine.

Thursday, February 18 Email to family from me
```
Family,
        Today nearly came and went without
any news regarding our latest MRI results.
BUT, I just got off the phone with Dr.
Brooks at 8:45 pm (hard-working guy). He
let us know that:
        1.      the corpus callosum was seen in
                its entirety.
        2.      there was no sign of blood on
                the brain (or hemorrhage).
```

3.   the lateral ventricles were
     confirmed as smaller than our
     last MRI (no measurement
     given).
4.   the third ventricle was normal
     sized.

He believes that these are good
results and mostly confirmed what we
expected. He advised us that we should
regard the Philly doc's prognosis (80-90%
"good") as our current status, considering
that all else has been deemed "normal" in
our case.

Perhaps needless to say, Dan and I
have decided that our pregnancy is going
to full term. We're having a boy!! Now we
can talk about names, the nursery, hand-
me-down clothes! Now we can talk freely to
Peyton about her brother. (BTW, Peyton
kissed and hugged my belly last night, her
own idea.) Oh, and I can start working on
Liko's baby quilt. We are so excited.
Hooray, hooray!

From here forward we need to consider
what kind of medical information we want.
Dr. Brooks suggested that we schedule an
ultrasound for two weeks to see how things
have progressed, and to discuss our plan
going forward. He'll propose his suggested
plan at that time for continued imaging,
and we'll need to have an idea of how much
we are willing to participate in (or would
we rather enjoy the pregnancy and follow
up with diagnostics after Liko is born?).

We are definitely continuing with
energy healing, yoga, and counseling. I'm
also meeting with a doula tomorrow
(specialized birthing coach).

Thanks for all of your positive
vibes, prayers, notes, calls, and
nurturing expressions. We are so lucky, in
SO many ways.

Love you all, Kelly

After writing this email, I sat back and noticed how similar my emailed family updates had been to those I had received from Rebecca just a few years before — filled with doctor names and medical terms and numbers that meant more to the author than to the recipients. Just as our story with Liko felt like a roller coaster, so did Rebecca's messages with her up-and-down news. As I reread the email, I sensed that the similarities with Rebecca would end here, that our son would be okay.

I marveled at our good fortune in this moment. *Why us?* Rebecca had been faithful, but we had never "turned to God" — though many of our family and friends did on our behalf. I wondered if the Prayer Warriors' prayers worked, or maybe it was Carol's healing energy light. Or maybe our practice of coming up with "wish lists" before each exam manifested the outcomes that we sought. *Did we speak his healing into existence?* But I'm sure Rebecca did all of those things, too. We had a good outcome and Rebecca had a terrible outcome, because…well, this is just life. I felt lucky and grateful we were here.

Our news about Liko on this day felt too high and too stable for me to consider that any lows could soon be possible — that, if there would be lows, surely they would be in the distant future as we watched Liko grow and develop.

But, two significant drops waited for us soon ahead.

Chapter 17

Labor

O ver the following weeks, Dan and I exhaled deeper into happiness and the routines of being expecting parents. I blissfully continued my pregnancy yoga classes, finally able to join the community of women who *knew* they were going to have a baby. With continued ultrasounds, by 28 weeks, Liko's ventricle measurements hit the *normal* range with 9mm. Dr. Sun, my OB, cautioned that Liko might arrive quickly.

"Your first baby came so quickly...just two and a half hours."

"Right, and a lot of pain," I remembered.

"Exactly," and he smiled sympathetically. "In my experience the second comes quicker."

"Is that even possible?" My mouth gaped.

"Oh, yes. I don't mean to be alarming, but this kid could drop in a parking lot on your way into the hospital."

"Jeez."

"Well, it *does* happen. I want you to be prepared in case it happens to you. Let's look into some classes on home birth for both you and your husband. I'd want you to try to get here, but if you can't, wherever you are, you'll know what to do."

"Are you kidding me?" And I giggled with joy.

"Absolutely not," and he smiled knowing that a quick birth would be welcome news compared to what we had been fearing just weeks earlier. *Oh, to have such problems. This is the life.*

"Sure we'll look into it. But the last pregnancy, well, Dan was just so tickled to be a dad, he could hardly think of all of the breathing techniques that he learned in our birthing class."

"Some people hire a doula. You could look into that. Dan could be free to be wrapped up in being a dad, and you'd have someone there who'd know what to do. But honestly, I just fear that even a doula wouldn't be able to get there in time. You'd need to head directly here and hope you make it."

The thought just made me giggle. What a cool birth story that would be for our son. However, I hired a doula anyway.

Journal Entry Monday, April 12 (31 weeks)

I had an emergency appointment at Dr. Sun's today. I've been leaking a clear watery discharge all day today. Soaked my pants all the way through, all day, especially when standing. I taught class tonight worrying about the spot on my pants. Dr. Sun is not sure what it is. He took a swab test that I'll get results for tomorrow. It will only tell me if I'm *not* likely to deliver within two weeks. I wonder if my bladder is leaking?? But it doesn't smell like pee. Dr. Sun thinks it's a discharge.

After writing in my journal that night, I turned to sleep. I woke at 12:30 am with wet pajamas. I changed my clothes, put a pad on and a towel under me, and went back to bed. I woke again at 1:30 am with the towel completely soaked through. This time I knew what it was. There was no mistaking.

I called the doula from the bathroom next to our bed as Dan slept. "I'm so sorry to wake you. I don't know what to do."

"What's going on?"

"Well, I'm nearly certain that my water broke, but I'm 31 weeks."

"Tell me what happened." And I told her about my day and the soaked through towel. "Yes, that's what it is, all right. You need to get to the hospital right now."

"The hospital? But I'm not having contractions."

"None?"

"No…well maybe. None that hurt. I've been having painless contractions for months. I did with my first pregnancy, too. I never thought much of them."

"Yeah, you still need to go to the hospital."

"Even if I'm not in labor?"

"Yes," she slowed her speaking. "As soon as your bag of waters breaks, you need to go in, no matter what else is happening. You are at risk for infection."

"Do you think I'm going into labor?"

"You just might."

"But I'm 31 weeks."

"I know," her voice was straight and honest. "They'll do everything they can to stop it. There's quite a lot they can do these days to slow it down. And they'll certainly try. But you have to get there now. Go ahead and go. Have Dan give me a call with an update when you're there. My guess is that they'll slow this down tonight, but please keep me updated."

"Okay, I sure will." And I hung up. *Oh my god. I have to go to the hospital. And right now.*

"Um, Dan, you've got to wake up."

"Huh, what?" He was annoyed. Having a toddler in our house meant that our sleep was precious.

"My towel soaked. We have to go to the hospital."

"Can you just get another towel?"

"No, I just called the doula. My water broke, so I have to go to the hospital. And now."

Dan jumped into action. He took our sleeping toddler to the neighbor's house, and I wrapped myself in a towel and sat calmly in the car. For my first child's birth, my trip to the hospital had been loud and painful, but this was quite different. The ride felt routine, like we were headed for an appointment, no rush, no breathing techniques. Once we pulled up to the hospital's late-night emergency entrance, the reality began to hit me. The concierge staff rushed to my side with a wheelchair.

I attempted to brush them off, "I can walk, thanks."

"Aren't you in labor?"

"Not really. I'm fine."

Dan tried to help, "No her water just broke, that's all. She's just 31 weeks, she's not in labor."

"Oh, no, if your water broke, you need to sit in this wheelchair."

"Okay, whatever you need me to do." They took me directly to the labor and delivery floor. "Am I having this baby?"

"Maybe ma'am. Maybe."

"But, I can't. I'm only 31 weeks." And my face cracked. My eyes filled. And my heart ached. *Again. This boy.*

"These are very good doctors. They'll try to help."

I didn't get it. I wasn't in labor. How was I supposed to have this baby? *They wouldn't dare induce a 31-week pregnancy, would they? A preemie. I'm going to have a preemie.* I didn't know much about preemies. I'd heard the word and knew what it meant, vaguely. *But how early was too early? Would he be born in the way I had envisioned at 24 weeks — my full labor and pushing, to give birth to a non-viable fetus? Is he going to die?*

A labor and delivery nurse came to get me from the concierge. He reported, "Her water broke."

And I filled in, "But I'm only 31 weeks." I sobbed loudly. "31 weeks! I'm going to have a preemie." I was devastated. All that angst just weeks before, and we were not going to get to know this guy after all.

"Not if we can help it," and she pushed me quickly down the hall to find an available L&D room. She gave me a pep talk as she glided me down the hall. "We've got to get you calm. You're going to do much better if you can calm yourself."

And I knew I could. *There's no decision for me to make this time. What will happen, will happen. I have no control. No guilt. I'm a spectator. We may be facing a life I had feared weeks earlier, but now I'm fully in for this life, wherever it goes.* I relaxed into my chair.

She set me up in room 326, and talked to Dan and me about the excellent care at the hospital. A neonatologist came to sit with us. She did an ultrasound, rigged me up to monitoring, and talked us through their plan.

"He looks like he's almost three pounds."

Ugh. I tried to picture him. *How big is that?* "Is that viable?"

"Our goal will be to make him more and more viable every hour."

"But how early is too early?"

"Oh. Well, the youngest preemies that we've been able to keep viable are about 26 weeks, but there are associated disabilities."

"How do you feel about 31 weeks?"

"I'd say it's about the middle. You're not super early, but not as far along as I'd like. It looks like your contractions are coming every three minutes and you are 1-2 centimeters dilated. So you *are* in labor and making progress."

"But, I still don't feel the contractions."

She smiled, "I guess that's a good thing. But, make no mistake, this is labor."

"Am I going to have this baby?"

"Well, you're not leaving this hospital until you do. Now if that's tonight or three weeks from now, time will tell. We'll do our best to keep him inside as long as we can. You are officially placed on hospital bed rest."

Whoa, but I have a job. I'm supposed to teach tomorrow. I wanted to save my sick days for my maternity leave. I have to take care of my family. My daughter! When will I see her? Dan! He'll be a solo dad. "No getting up at all?"

"You can go to the bathroom and maybe shower, but that's it."

"For three weeks?"

"Ideally, yes. Development wise, he'd be viable enough at 34 weeks. So we'll try to keep him in that long. But labor is powerful. He'll come when he comes, and we *do* have ways to slow things down. Literally every hour counts. New developments are constantly happening for a fetus. What we're concerned about right now, with you at 31 weeks, is his lung development. His lungs just aren't ready yet. This is a key issue for preemies. We have a steroid shot that we can give you that is very effective at speeding along fetal lung development. It comes in two doses that are given 24 hours apart. So we need to do our best to keep this guy inside you for at least 48 hours."

"How can you keep the labor from taking over?"

"Magnesium sulfate is a powerful muscle relaxer and can be very effective at slowing labor. We'll administer that intravenously. Some patients report a side effect of a burning sensation."

"Bring it on." Nurses set me up with an IV and started the mag to slow contractions and an antibiotic to ward off infection. Another nurse came in to give the steroid shot in my thigh. At first I could feel the pain of the shot, and I moaned expecting the pain to subside as quickly as it came. But then, I could feel the steroid collect in my leg and burn. The pain didn't go away. I knew the exact boundaries of where the steroid sat inside my leg, because the pain pulsed there. "Ow, ow! It won't stop hurting."

"Yeah, it's a powerful medicine. You'll feel relief when it dissipates."

"I thought the mag is the one that's supposed to burn."

"Oh, it can, too, but it's more of a build-up."

"It's *still* hurting. Ugh. I honestly think that's the worst shot I've ever had."

"Yeah, I've heard that before."

"And I have to have another one of these?"

"Yes, in 24 hours exactly."

"I am *not* looking forward to that!" And I tried to shake off the thought.

After we settled into our room and the medical routine, the neonatologist returned. "Your mag is working, your contractions have slowed and it looks as though they've even stopped. I feel confident that we'll get both steroid dosages in."

"What's our prognosis?"

"He *is* small, but our plan is working so far. It's just too hard to tell with changes happening every hour. If he were to be born this week, at 31 weeks, there are chances of a wide range of disabilities."

That sounds familiar; we've heard this before.

"Unfortunately, White males tend to have more complications than girls and Polynesian and Asian babies." We had heard this before, too. She raised an eyebrow, "But you are in good hands here. If you had gone to another hospital, they would have sent you here. And you came here first, so you have the benefit of an early response to your situation."

Thanks, but I hear what you're not saying. You're not saying that we'll all be okay.

For the next couple of days the mag held off my contractions, and the steroids did their magic. I tried to teach my classes on-line from my computer, much to the chagrin of my nurses. Eventually, they had me turn the computer off. Mostly, I passed the time with visitors. Dan and Peyton came before her bedtime, and also friends, coworkers, and hospital staff kept me company. One boisterous older nurse enjoyed telling me stories of the hospital.

"You know Obama was born here, right?"

"Oh? I thought he was born in Kenya," I said with a joking smirk.

"Ha!" She cracked up. "True, I must be mistaken," she looked at me sideways with a chuckle.

"But seriously," I wondered, "in this very hospital?"

"Absolutely!"

"I didn't know that."

"And, actually, Cher's been here, too. I was here that night."

"No way."

"Way!"

"Did she give birth? Was it Chas....or, um, I mean Chaz? He's about my age, so like the early 1970s?"

"Oh, no, I'm not that old. Must have been after that?"

"Right."

"I tell you what though; you are in good hands here. I wouldn't worry too much about a preemie. Many perfectly healthy and successful people were preemies. Once you are in that world, you pay more attention. They are everywhere."

"Really, I don't think I know any preemies."

"Oh, I'm sure you do."

A young physician was in the room checking my meds and charts. "I was a preemie."

The nurse lit up, "That's right. I had forgotten that. And, um, Dr. Isaki, too. Right?"

"Right. Oh, there's a lot of us. Dr. Young, Dr. Aikau, Dr. Halagao... I think there's something about having been a preemie that drives us to want to become physicians."

That was nice to hear. I started to feel encouraged.

Once when Dan was visiting, a new nurse popped into my room to check vitals. She was very friendly, "Oh it's so nice to have folks like you two in here."

"Oh yeah? Like us how?" *Do you mean, nice 'n White?*

"You know, clean and thin."

"Clean?" *Do you mean, nice 'n not poor?*

"Yeah," and she lowered her voice to a whisper, "we get folks here from Waianae Coast," and she gestured down the hall. "Dey come in here dirty with bugs and bad health. En dey fat. Hard to run tests wit all dat fat." *Great. Nothing like a hospital worker who only wants to work with healthy people. Come on Lady.*

I was disgusted by her, "Well I'm glad they can get such good care here."

And that seemed to shut her up. *Please don't engage me in small talk about your biases, and while you're at it, rethink your profession.*

A show-boating physician who I'd never met came in with a posse of three young residents to tell me that it was her informed opinion that I shouldn't be on the mag. "Studies show that it's not actually effective at slowing labor."

"But my labor did slow."

"My reading of your charts indicated that your labor never really got going."

"Then what's the harm?"

"There's no harm, but there are side effects that you can avoid. I hear your arm is burning."

"What am I supposed to do? Decide I don't want this? I didn't order it. If you have a concern about my care, shouldn't you talk to my doctor about it?"

"I wanted you to know, to keep you informed."

My God lady. I am not sleeping well in here. My kid might be born with some problems. I'm trying to stay calm and healthy. Don't bother me with this. "Please, if you are concerned, talk to my OB, Dr. Sun. I trust him." And they all left.

Later in the day Dr. Sun came by to joke that the results of my Monday swab indicated that I would likely go into labor within the week. I laughed, "Ya don't say! And so much for the quick birth in a parking lot, too!"

"Yeah, right! Also, I talked to Dr. Raimondo." He smirked. "Technically, she's right. There isn't conclusive evidence that the mag works."

"Look, I just want to trust you right now. The labor did stop, maybe because of the mag. I don't care. If you wanted to try this, and it seems to have worked, then I'm fine. I just didn't want her bothering me for my medical opinion. I've got other things on my mind right now. If she had new information that she felt was persuasive, then I wanted her to talk with you, and I'll just do what you say. So, if you're fine with this, so am I."

Dr. Brooks came by later to let me know that my early labor was most likely not related to our earlier pregnancy issues. *Gosh, the thought hadn't even occurred to me.* "Oh I didn't know that was a thing."

"Well, but it's not really. When our team got the news that you were in here, the thought crossed our minds. We had a meeting and reviewed your case. We think these are unrelated."

Wow, you had a meeting about us?

"And I heard that Dr. Raimondo stopped by?" He smirked, too. I nodded. "Ya know, this is her research area, and I think she's made an interesting contribution there, but mag to slow a preemie is standard practice. It's just what we do." I felt that I was in capable hands.

After 24 hours with my second steroid shot, the pain from the mag in my arm was unbearable. They removed the mag and expected my labor to return in full force shortly.

We were looking at an April 15 birthday for our boy, and that felt odd. *Tax day. How boring? What if he's an accountant? That could be stressful for him. Well, I guess he could celebrate after his big deadline. Or maybe his partner shouldn't be an accountant, because the accountant wouldn't be able to plan anything special for his birthday. Too busy with work. Wait, is he going to be okay?* But the labor took more than a day to manifest.

After four days in the hospital on strict bedrest, I was exhausted and had no energy to be in labor. Between the round-the-clock hourly checks of my vitals and the beeping machines, restful sleep was impossible. I needed meds. Contractions did pick up, and I quickly requested an epidural. The pain staved off a bit, but I still felt it. I was so NOT in the mood for pain. I felt numbness in my lungs if I slouched too low, but sitting up took effort especially when the contractions came. As is often the case after an epidural, the contractions slowed, so then I was given Pitocin, the drug that picks things up again. I learned from giving birth to my first child exactly how I needed to push. Between that knowledge and our son's small size, he was out in two pushes.

I had been preoccupied enough with wishing away tax day as his birthday that it didn't occur to me that April 16 would be a "death day" birthday for my son, the third anniversary of the massacre at Virginia Tech, my alma mater.

And so, that was when he was born.

My son and I were both born on death dates, and his birth story included more hints at death than mine ever did. I recalled that Carol, the energy healer, said we had an old connection and that already felt true to me, that maybe we would travel similar life paths. *How old will he be when he experiences his first peer death? Will he become as preoccupied with death as I had been? Can I teach him that death is not about him, or is that a better lesson learned on his own?*

But his connection to death would continue much sooner than I could imagine.

Chapter 18

Danny

D aniel Chilton Merrill, Jr. was born at 12:30 pm. He was quickly taken to a table across my room with the neonatal team. From my view, he looked purple. Dan was with him and cut his umbilical cord. He noticed Danny's concave chest, and a nurse mentioned that that was typical of preemies. Another nurse strapped a breathing mask on his face, bundled him, and brought him to me for a brief visit. She asked me to hold the mask to his face and give him a sideways welcome-to-the-world hug as she would continue to hold him. He looked reddish pink now, not purple any more. Dan followed the neonatal team and Danny to the newborn intensive care unit (NICU). He weighed three and a half pounds.

It was about five hours before I was allowed to visit Danny in the NICU in my wheelchair. Dan had already left to take care of our toddler at home; this first visit was just me and my nurse. The NICU was a secure room with a punch-code door and a staffed sign-in desk. A sign read, "Access Controlled, No one under age 15." *Oh, so Peyton can't visit.* After signing in, I was instructed to wash my hands in a very particular way. A poster outlined the steps. *This* soap; then rinse. *This* scrub, this far down both arms; then rinse. *This* drying towel. The room was large with rows and rows of tiny hospital beds and incubators on wheels. Several beeping machines were attached to each bed. Families pulled up cheap plastic rolling office chairs to be near the baby they were visiting. Nurses buzzed between a few babies each.

Danny was the second from the last row to the right, in the second to last bed on the right. Danny was in an incubator with stickers on his face and body that were holding wires and tubes in place. His breathing mask was strapped on over his tiny head; we could hardly see his face. He had dark brown hair that laid smooth against his head. Danny's primary NICU nurse, Cynthia, allowed me to hold him for a bit but she emphasized that being held took energy from him. Nurse Cynthia handed him to me in a tightly wrapped bundle, careful to lay his wires and tubes to the side so they'd stay connected to the machines. *Hi, I'm your mom. Good to finally meet you.* His eyes stayed closed as I studied his face. *What color are your eyes?* Holding Danny was brief and infrequent. He needed all the energy he had for developing, growing, and surviving.

After just two more nights of recovery, I was discharged from the hospital on a Sunday. I felt guilty for not being home for nearly a week and leaving Dan to fly solo with our toddler. I was determined to go to the zoo for a family adventure day. I insisted that it really wasn't that big of a deal on my body to give birth to a preemie. Only when we were there did I realize my body's organs were still trying to find their way back to their original pre-pregnancy positions. Walking around wasn't such a great idea.

Conveniently, the hospital was close to both home and work. Dan and I would both visit 3-4 times a day, sometimes together if our toddler was in day care, but often separately. The closeness of the babies in the NICU meant that we saw others' experiences up-close. I saw two circumcisions performed. A boy on one side of us had an unusually small pointed skull and a tracheotomy. I gathered from overhearing discussions of social workers near him that the mother would not visit and likely did not want him. Another boy, younger than Danny, was huge, appearing to weigh at least 15 pounds. His sign said that he had been born just a few days earlier at seven pounds. I learned from overhearing others that he was born at home and didn't breathe. The midwife called EMTs who arrived with a shot that made him swell from the medicine. Most other babies in the NICU appeared to be standard preemies on track for good health.

Over the next few days Danny's condition was stable and encouraging. Any concerns were minor and improved easily. His color improved to reveal that he was jaundiced, which was easily improved with lamp time in his incubator. A brain ultrasound revealed a grade 1 brain bleed, not a big deal we were told. His breathing improved, and he was demoted to an oxygen tube across his nose. I enjoyed the brief times I was allowed to hold him, sometimes even skin-to-skin, called kangaroo care. I was taught how to feed him through the gavage feeding tube, associating my presence with his full belly. I changed his diaper, which was a challenge since his butt had NO fat. He looked like a skinny old man to me–like Benjamin Buttons. Dan would visit Danny with his favorite book, *Ender's Game*. He'd read to Danny just so Danny could hear his voice. I didn't know how to talk to him. I tried, but mostly I'd just stare and hold his hand. He'd clutch hard onto my finger. It was hard to leave him there when it was time for me to go home.

After Danny was a week old, we learned the vocabulary of "apneas" and "bradys," often shortened to "As and Bs." Apneas were moments when Danny stopped breathing. Brady was a nickname for bradycardia, an abnormal slowing of the heart. Danny would have a few episodes of As and Bs here and there, each one signaled with beeping machines. This happened enough that Dan and I both learned the terms and were also assured that these weren't a big deal, just a relic of an immature human body learning what it needs to do to live. "Preemies just do this." One Monday evening after Dan was at the NICU visiting Danny and I was home attending to Peyton, he returned gut-wrenched.

I greeted Dan with a smile when he got home, "How was he?"

Dan looked at me briefly, then at the ground and shook his head, "Man, the As and Bs were bad tonight. It's just so hard for me to see."

I brushed it off, "Yeah, they say it's not that big of a deal though."

"But it was a lot tonight, Kelly. *A lot.*"

"Like how much?"

"They were calling them *extreme* bradys tonight, and I counted six apneas in just 15 minutes. Once a nurse even ran over to him and rubbed his forehead pretty aggressively to bring him back. He even had blue lips."

"Whoa, but the rubbing worked?"

"I guess. They continued to play it off like it's normal, but the nurse did admit that it was a lot more often than his usual."

"Did it calm back down before you left?"

"Maybe? Not really. It just didn't matter that I was there. I felt in the way."

When we visited the next few days his condition seemed back to normal with occasional As and Bs. But, four days later we'd receive the worst phone call of our lives.

Saturday, May 1 at 4:30 a.m., Dan's phone rang. We both woke.

"It's the NICU," and he answered it. "Hello. This is him. Yes. Right. Oh. What does that mean? Should we come? When? Thanks."

"What is it?"

"This is bad, Kelly." He leaned back, crammed his fists in his eyes, let out a sigh, and grabbed his hair with both hands.

"What is it?"

"They think he has meningitis."

"I've heard of it, and know it's bad, but I don't even know what it is."

"Yeah, me too. They said it's a brain infection. They won't know the results for another 24 hours, but in the meantime, they have him on a bunch of antibiotics. They think it probably started Monday with all of the As and Bs, and they only now just got him on antibiotics. This is bad."

He just sat there stunned and I was confused. "Should we go to be with him?"

"No, no. They said we shouldn't come until 7:30am, after the shift change. They said they are too busy with him now, lots to do, and stuff we shouldn't see. They need to do a spinal tap. Apparently that's pretty brutal to watch."

We sat there stunned. Sleep was over. We were up, and our daughter wasn't — a rare moment. I wanted to learn more about meningitis. I picked up my cell phone and searched through sites to learn what I could. *How bad is this?*

I read that newborn meningitis is pretty bad. That it mattered what kind of bug he was infected with, which we wouldn't find out for some time. But generally, he had equal chances of death, disability, or "normalcy" — 33% chance for each. *God, we're here in this place again — thinking about our son and death and disability again.* And somehow, as concerned as I was, I was able to relax into knowing that I was powerless.

I called my mother and father to update them. I feared the worst happening and me having to tell them the whole story from the beginning. I wanted to prepare them now. Dan didn't call his family, trusting that he'd be able to tell them about all of this once we knew that it would all be okay.

Dan, Peyton, and I all arrived together at the hospital at 7:30 a.m. The plan was that I'd go into the NICU first, while Dan and Peyton waited in the lobby, then we'd switch. Danny wasn't in his usual spot. I was led farther down past the end of incubator rows to a new room within the NICU. This was the room for the toughest cases. Danny was spread out motionless on a raised and small flat-bed, not the incubator. Warm lights shone on him for heat. His head was covered with a blanket and wires and tubes strung all about from under the blanket and over his body. He had his own exclusive nurse in this room. I asked, "What's the blanket for?"

"He's sensitive to light because of the infection. Are you Mom?"

"Yes. I am. He's not moving."

"Right. I'll see if I can find the doctor on call to talk with you." She left. While she was gone, I wanted to hold Danny's hand, but there was an IV there. I wanted to hold his foot, but there was a clamp on it. *Oh, he's bloody.* Blood was smeared over his legs. I noticed that his legs had a nice shape. They looked like baby soccer player legs. I imagined him 16 on the high school soccer team and me watching from the sidelines. *Am I in denial? Is that what I'm doing?* His machines continued to beep and I could see that he was having As and Bs. When the nurse returned she attended to the beeping machines.

The duty neonatologist found me. "Hi, you're Mom?"

"Yes."

"Last night was pretty eventful for Danny."

"Yes, we were told."

"I'm just getting on duty, so I'll catch you up as best as I can. He had sepsis, an infection in his blood stream. What makes that very serious is that it carries the infection all over the body to other systems. So, we know the infection made it to the brain. The spinal tap was clearly positive for meningitis. Now we just need to figure out what bug he has so we can use the right strategy to get it. He's on a strong antibiotic cocktail now that will kill most things. We can back off on that when we know exactly which he needs. We're also in the process of figuring out what other systems have been infected."

"He's bloody."

"Yes, we put in a PICC line," she grimaced, "to administer the medications more quickly."

I don't know what a PICC line is but it sounds serious.

"He also had a few bicycling seizures this morning. So we've been monitoring his brain activity and started an anti-seizure med, too."

Seizures, too? My God! This keeps getting worse. "He's not moving."

"Right."

Right? That's all you can say? I knew things were bad.

"Can our daughter meet him? She's not even two, so I know it's against the rules. But if we lose him," and my eyes welled up, "she's going to have a better shot of dealing with it," and my voice creaked on my words, so I whispered the rest "if she can meet him." Then I took a deep breath.

"Oh, so, you know how serious this is."

Oh wow, she knows, and she knows I know. She's not trying to talk me down. I'm not being unreasonable. My voice got clearer and my tears faded, "Can she just meet him through some window? Like, can we wheel him over to a window where she can see him? She needs to meet her brother." And I cried again.

And her eyes filled, too. "I really don't think so, but I'll check."

While she left I noticed that Danny's nurse had been attending to him through his continuing As and Bs. I hoped that I could help. I rubbed the side of his head through the blanket, and there was beeping. I decided to hold his leg and rub slightly. And the machines beeped. So the rubbing didn't work. I stopped rubbing and gently held his leg instead. But there was beeping. I held his toe. Beeping. I backed off entirely. No touching. Beeping. Nothing I did, or didn't do, made any bit of difference. He looked so miserable, and I couldn't help. *I am helpless. This is all up to him now.*

The duty doctor returned, "We can't move Danny. He needs to stay right where he is and not expend any energy other than healing."

"I understand," and I moved toward the door.

"Oh, you are welcome to stay," she motioned for me to return.

"I really can't." I shook my head and looked down. I sensed judgement, and it was coming from me. I rationalized, "I'm helpless here. I think my husband will come up next, though. He's with our daughter in the lobby now." I walked out of the NICU area quickly with tears streaming, careful not to sob and careful not to wipe the tears. Other families in the NICU were nearby, wondering if their babies would make it, and I had to be brave for them. My wet face felt like a badge of honor. *These tears are for my son, and I am not ashamed.* But as soon as I got out into the hallways of the hospital, my determination to find Dan and Peyton replaced my tears.

I found them in the lobby, Dan walking behind Peyton as she explored every nook of the room, and every person who would make eye contact with her. I asked Dan, "Do you want to go see Danny next?"

"How does he look? I'm not sure if I can stand it."

"Honestly, he looks bad. His head is covered with a blanket because of the light sensitivity. His body is bloody from getting the needles in. The As and Bs are going crazy. I felt helpless."

"Yeah, I can't see him. It's just too hard. You can fill me in."

"It's bad, Dan. What if this is the last time you see him? Are you okay with that? This is a serious question. I'm not overreacting. The duty doctor was clear about this. He could die." And my tears were back. Peyton ran out of the lobby toward the elevators, thus demanding that we follow her while continuing our conversation.

"Yeah, I don't think I can."

"So, do you want to go home?"

"Yeah, I don't know what else to do."

"Okay. You don't need to go in, but I think you need to call your parents. I've already called mine. If Danny doesn't make it, your folks need to be prepared. And, we'd be so overwhelmed with grief we couldn't give them the backstory. You need to tell them now."

He agreed. As our family of three headed to the front door to exit, Dan dialed his cell phone to tell his parents the update. I tried to hold Peyton's hand to give Dan some space, but she sensed her daddy's need in that moment. Peyton reached up to her daddy, and Dan tried to carry her and hold the phone at the same time.

"Hello! Yes. Well. We're at the hospital now. No, not visiting Danny. Well, Kelly did. Actually, we got a call last night." And then he cracked. And not just his voice.

I had known Dan for seven years at this moment in 2010, and I had only seen him cry once. He was a movie fan, and back when we were dating he had never seen *Babe*, a movie about a talking pig who worked to fit in on a farm among the herding dogs. I thought it was a cute movie, and I insisted that he see it. At first he thought it was just clever, then the story drew him in more. By the final scene, when the pig competed in a herding contest, Dan was engaged. He laughed aloud as he cheered for Babe. The last line of the movie must have been perfection to him, "That'll do, Pig," because he shed tears through his smiling eyes. And that was the only time I'd ever seen him cry. Never out of sadness or frustration. Just utter joy, and only once.

But this time, as we exited the hospital and Dan held his phone in one hand and his adoring squirming toddler in the other, he collapsed. His voice collapsed. The breath in his lungs collapsed. His knees buckled. He put Peyton down as the tears started to roll in. We were outside in the loving Hawaiian air, but surrounded by tall concrete structures — the hospital, admin building, and parking deck. People walked in and out of the hospital. He felt exposed and embarrassed. I tried to hold onto

Peyton to give Dan his space. With the phone to his ear, Dan retreated back toward the hospital, but realized he didn't want to go back inside. He found a crevice between concrete faux columns that he tucked behind and slid against the walls, still trying to explain, "It doesn't look good. He might not make it." He crouched to the ground, and touched the cement to keep from falling. He was weak from too much energy leaving him at once.

Peyton reached for her daddy, "Why's Daddy crying?"

"He's very sad, honey."

"Why?"

"Baby brother is sick; and it is sad. Very sad."

We crouched down with Daddy and all shared a family hug as Dan continued to fill in his family. "We just don't know yet. I guess the next day or so we'll find out more. Yes, I'll let you know what we learn. Thanks so much. I know. That means a lot. I love you, too."

Dan wiped his eyes. "Wow, that was tough," and we walked to the car.

"Yes it is. This is very hard. And saying it is hard."

"Kelly, I think this is the worst day of my life."

"Wow, yeah. That makes sense. It is."

"Is it for you?"

"Good question. I don't think it is. I think that day has already passed. The pregnancy was harder for me, I think."

"Really? But we've been through all of that and might lose him anyway!"

"Yeah, I'm not saying this isn't hard. It is. I just think the decision we thought we had to make during pregnancy was much harder. It turned out that we didn't have to make that decision. But there were solid weeks that we didn't know that. Those were probably the worst days of my life. Any one of those in there would have qualified."

"I guess none of those days felt like an imminent threat to me. Like there was always just the *idea* that he wouldn't make it. And now, it's a reality. Like, it could be happening right now." We both looked at his phone. *Is it happening right now?*

"But this time, I don't feel responsible. Either he is going to make it or he isn't. This is his work to do. There's nothing we can do about it. Before, when I was pregnant, I was much more responsible for what happened to him."

"And I guess I didn't feel that way."

"I know." *I wanted you to, but you didn't. So now, maybe, we're emotionally even.*

"Well, let's hope it doesn't get much worse than this. I think this is about all I can take."

"Yeah, one day at a time."

With a toddler we had no choice but to settle into familiar routines; our sadness was sidelined. Peyton's consciousness just wasn't in a place where she could understand what was happening. She obviously continued to have physical and emotional needs and we did our best to be there for her.

Sunday, May 2, 2010, Journal Entry, Danny is 2 weeks old today

Today, we got the official word that Danny has meningitis caused by two bugs, e coli and enterococcus. Yuck. From what we gather, prognosis is equal for death, disability, and normalcy. But, we are told that Danny "looks" much better today than yesterday. He's crying, his color is good. Yesterday he had several (over 3) seizures all in the morning. The neurologist ordered an EEG for Monday to see his brain activity and an MRI "later" to assess the "damage."

Today and tomorrow he's getting blood transfusions @ 17ccs per day. Apparently he's lost a lot of blood from all of the testing they are doing. (I saw a staffer get chewed out about this.) I'm feeling encouraged today.

Friends and neighbors rallied to our side with prepared meals and offers to watch Peyton. I understood and appreciated their care, but didn't feel it was necessary. We had nothing to do but wait for news. There was solace in our routines. We had nothing to mourn yet, but the meals made it seem that we should be mourning already. The best expressions of care were friends who would sit with us, hear our story, and talk through hypotheticals.

My mother, who had just recently retired, decided to catch an earlier flight out to come see us. She had planned to arrive for Danny's birth in mid-June, but as a preemie, his due date was still well over a month in the future. Her earlier arrival would be just what we needed.

Wednesday, May 5, 2010, Journal Entry, Danny is 2 weeks old and 5 days

Dr. Ong says Danny has survived, so now we'll be concerned about disability caused from brain damage. That could take years to fully understand. But there is some testing they can begin once he's off antibiotics (3 weeks), EEG and MRI.

I'm feeling great – very positive and optimistic!! Dan is getting there. I got to hold Danny for the first time in nearly a week (last was Thursday).

May 5ᵗʰ is Boys' Day in Japan and is celebrated in Hawai'i by households flying carp-shaped windsocks outside their homes to represent how many boys live there. That day a colleague gave me a Boys' Day greeting card with a paper cutout of a blue carp, and a congratulatory note about the arrival of our son. This was the day we knew he'd survived, so we knew that Boys' Day would continue to be a holiday we celebrated with enthusiasm for years to come.

Before Danny was born, I went to the hospital an average of three times a week for appointments and testing – blood work, ultrasounds, amnio test, MRI, EKG, counseling, OB-GYN, and neurologist opinion. But after he was born, I was going at least three times a day. Certainly, though, being at the hospital that frequently for several months straight was not good for my scholarly productivity. Professors are made and broken based on their scholarly productivity. I *did* have a research paper accepted at a competitive conference that I was prepared to deliver in late April. *AND* a reporter from a popular academic newspaper had contacted me in advance of the conference to show interest in writing a story about my findings. That would have been excellent for my reputation as an academic. But, Danny was born just a week before the conference and I was unable to attend and deliver the paper.

As the nurses worked to train Danny toward breastfeeding, my presence was more critical to his wellbeing. From the moment he was born, I was pumping breast milk so that I would continue to produce it. I brought it into the hospital for the nurses to feed him through a gavage tube. Given my experience with Peyton, I knew that my milk productivity can be low, so I was thrilled with physical evidence of my milk supply. I could see it with my own eyes, instead of wondering how much was inside my baby's belly. Since I was either pumping at home or directly breastfeeding Danny at the hospital every three hours, my days were segmented into one-hour outings. It took me about an hour to relax into and provide the actual breastfeeding. Then, I could count on my leaving and returning to take a half-hour on each end, so anywhere I was headed I would only be there an hour, then I'd need to go. No getting caught up in conversations. Grocery shopping had to take one hour, visits to my office to get work supplies had to take one hour. Any errand could only take one hour. If it took more, I'd have to leave and continue it during my next free hour. And I was continuing to teach three graduate courses at this time. I had planned my due date so as to not interfere with my teaching duties, but I hadn't planned on a preemie. I couldn't take sick days because I needed them for my maternity leave that I had planned for the fall, so I could teach less than usual then. It would be much better to teach classes while juggling a newborn baby who's mostly being watched by a hospital staff, than it would be to juggle a six-month-old without childcare.

During one of my one-hour breaks, the chair of my department insisted that I needed a doctor's note to return to campus, though I had already been teaching after birth. I explained that I was fine and could return to work. She explained that it's an HR policy and I would just have to do what I'm told, though I recalled no such requirement after my daughter was born. She also was clear that this letter needed to be on file as soon as possible, as I was already putting the university at risk. I had no idea what type of note they needed, and couldn't get much clarification from my chair. But it was time to breastfeed, so I had to go. During my next hour on campus, three hours later, I visited an HR representative to get more clarification about what I needed. They were very kind and patient. The letter was a requirement, but it didn't seem as urgent from their perspective. From the HR office, I called the OB-GYN's office to ask for precisely what I needed, a letter explaining that although I've given birth recently, I am able to come to campus and do my job without any threat to my health. At my next breastfeeding visit at the hospital, I was able to pick up the letter, only to discover that they had misunderstood my request. The letter explained that I should be allowed to stay away from work. *NO!* I explained to the folks at the OB-GYN office; they understood and agreed to make a new letter, but it would be a couple hours before the doctor would be available to do so. I returned to campus without my letter.

The chair was furious at me for coming on campus *again* without a proper letter on file. She was annoyed with me. I was *extremely* annoyed at her for having *NO* understanding for what I might be going through. She lit into me, and I left. I was emotionally fragile enough. I didn't need her anger for something so trivial. I said, "I know you need to be angry about this, but I don't need to be, so I need to go." And I boldly just walked away. I did have a good explanation, but I didn't have time or patience for explaining things. I wanted her support and I wanted her to trust that there *was* an explanation and that I was working on it, but she didn't. Eventually I did get my letter in.

About a week later, I was at a university event where my dean was in attendance leaning on a cane. She had heard the news of my son's birth adventures through my husband. She told me the story of her own son's eventful birth, which almost took her own life. She also told me that just a few weeks earlier, when I was in the hospital, she had a knee replacement surgery. We were probably in the same hospital at the same time. She explained, "In fact, the HR office is still on me to give them a letter explaining that I'm okay to be back on campus again. Have you ever heard of such a thing?"

"Actually, yes, they got on me about the same thing," and we shared a chuckle. But, as I spoke with the dean, I left out the detail that the pressure was actually coming from my chair and not the HR office. Given that my dean and I were in the hospital at the same time, and she had not yet turned in a letter, the conversation confirmed for me that it was my chair, not HR, who had over-reacted to my situation.

Danny would be on his antibiotics for 21 days. His weight improved to four pounds, then over a week later to five pounds. He continued to have spinal taps and blood tests to monitor the infection. The results were on track, but the healing would take time. He had an MRI and a video EEG to monitor his brain activity. His seizures had stopped, though he was on an anti-seizure med. The MRI showed scarring on his brain. I had read that brain scars are a result of seizures, and can even initiate more seizures – creating a potential cycle for brain damage.

My friends threw me a post-birth baby shower since Danny had arrived too early for a traditionally timed shower. They were gracious to get me out of the work – hospital – toddler-care cycle. They selected a lovely tea room back in the Manoa Valley of Honolulu. We sat on an outdoor lanai in a rainforest area, with large vine trees surrounding us with their sweet fragrances. We wore cute little sun dresses, sipped tea, and breathed the warm moist air in deeply. *I needed this.*

They wondered aloud, "How is he doing?"

"He looks pretty good, actually. We're pleased," and I forced a smile.

They smiled politely. "Oh good," and I could see they had more questions in their eyes. *Could he still die? Is he disabled? How are you sitting here? How are you doing any of this?*

This all feels familiar. I've been here before. I suddenly had an awareness that I was on the other side now. I used to have that look on my face back in Chicago when I didn't know how to have conversations with Nick about his cancer. I had the same questions for Miriam about how she could mourn for Nick. But now my friends were looking at me that way.

I had no idea myself. I had many of those same questions, even as I sat there and enjoyed their company and the peace of the tea room location. "You know, I think we're just in this place right now where, Danny's in the clear for now, and what the future holds we may not know for another few years. So here we are, enjoying where we are now. And it's good right now. I have two kids, one of them a newborn who of course doesn't sleep through the night, but he's being watched by the most amazing medical staff. I couldn't ask for anything better for him. And Dan and I are sleeping through the night. We have many of the perks of having a newborn, without sleepless nights, though, Peyton still wakes us at 6:00 a.m. every morning." And I smiled. *I have the good fortune of knowing my toddler. She's an early bird, and I get to know that about her. I hope I get to know Danny.*

Mother's Day came and went without my boy home. The daily challenge of keeping the household going, visiting the hospital multiple times, and maintaining professional jobs wore us down. Both Dan and I got sick with colds, but fortunately not at the same time. Dan necessarily stayed away from the NICU for one week, and then just as he returned to visit Danny again, I had to step away due to my cold. Fortunately my mother had arrived, so she fed Danny my stored-up breast milk as I stayed home and continued to pump and rest.

Friday, May 28 Journal Entry, Danny's 6 weeks old today
We waited all morning and into the early afternoon before we got word from the NICU (after getting the infectious disease doc's opinion). Danny can go home today! Hooray!

I emailed and texted family and friends, called Dan to set up a plan for picking him up at 4 p.m. We picked up Peyton at daycare and told her all about it. "We're going to take Danny home!"

Dan and I went into the NICU, and my mom and Peyton waited outside in the hallway. Nurse Patty said I could change his diaper one last time in the NICU. I leaned over to Patty just before changing his diaper and said, "I'm just waiting for someone to say 'no, he can't go home.'" I opened Danny's diaper and his scrotum looked very big to me. One of the neonatologists came up to me to say "Congrats for leaving" and I showed her. Before I knew it, Danny was surrounded by doctors. They thought it was a hernia from the area where his testicle was still working its way down. They tried to push it back, but it wouldn't go and Danny was fussy. That made them think he might need surgery on the spot. They called for a surgeon to come examine, but it would be a 2-hour wait. So they sent us home. The staff there was so sad for us to hear about the delay. Some nurses told me that Danny was becoming the cutie-pie favorite. Guess he gets to hang out with them more.

So we all went back home. Peyton didn't seem fazed that Danny wasn't coming with us. After dinner and Peyton's bedtime, we got a phone call that Danny didn't need surgery, and it wasn't the scary kind of hernia, but just a lot of fluid (12ccs) from his abdomen which drained down into his scrotum; a hydrocele. But, they did want to keep him for the night.

So here we are, at home, without Danny...

Through our time in the NICU we learned that there's a bit of a culture to the experience. Our lives revolved around the twice-daily shift change at 7:00 a.m. and p.m., and around the 3-hour feeding schedules. We knew being touched spent energy, and not to count on being allowed to touch our babies. We used words like kangaroo, bradys, As and Bs, CCs, and VM, with fluid ease. We knew how to read medical journals, "the *n* is too low." From this experience, I finally learned what "clinical" meant to the medical staff (observable or practical), which made my former title as clinical faculty member in an education school in Chicago make more sense. Spiritually, we learned that each day mattered, not only to our son's growth and development but to survival. The present was all any of us ever had. Each day marked how deeply this experience would work itself into our identities. Every NICU parent I met spoke in terms of days, "How many days have you been here?" And every parent talked in terms of us all being in the NICU, not just our babies. With their newborn consciousness, the NICU was more our experience than theirs.

Had we left the NICU on the day that he was first scheduled, on Friday, May 28, we would have been there a solid six weeks, or 42 days in NICU-speak. Fortunately, we were only delayed a day. We tried again on that Saturday. Dan and I brought along my mother and Peyton. Dan and I entered the NICU to say our goodbyes to the staff and to get our car seat inspected for fit with our exceptionally small child. I felt happiness in my face and peace as we moved through our tasks for dismissal. I wanted to remember this place. It had certainly shaped us. And it had nurtured us, too. I trusted that what was about to happen was supposed to happen. If we were stopped again, it would be frustrating, but necessary. Dan carried Danny in his car seat carrier, while we were escorted out by Danny's duty nurse, Sarah. For the first time, we walked out of the NICU *with* our son! Sunlight shown on him from the large hallway windows. Everything felt bigger, brighter, and open, even though I had been in that same space just moments earlier. Mom and Peyton were at the end of the hallway exploring the patterned colored tiles. Mom brought Peyton to us to meet her brother, and I got out my camera. Peyton walked right up to him, as if she had met him before, "Hello Danny," and she reached out and touched his leg. She continued along in her toddler world as if nothing just changed; though everything had. "Let's take Danny home!"

Danny had several follow-up medical appointments. He had a special round of respiratory disease vaccinations for preemies that required us to go in for a couple shots each week for several weeks. One of the antibiotics he had been on had a side effect of deafness, so we returned to the hospital for an infant hearing test. He passed. At five months, Danny had one more brain MRI that showed some residual brain healing and was otherwise normal. Dr. Tai, the pediatric neurologist, warned that due to his medical history, Danny was at risk for cerebral palsy and recommended infant yoga and massage. So Danny and I did those together. Not only did Danny survive his birth dramas, all signs indicated that he'd live a "typical" life. Danny met his gross motor milestones on the late end of normal: at seven months he could roll over, ten months he could sit up, eleven months he could crawl. He wouldn't walk until we were living in Virginia and he was 17 months old. He said his very first word the next day. Once Danny walked we could see what had been holding him back. He pronated his feet and ankles severely because he didn't trust his balance, and likely had some sort of balance disorder. His Virginia physical therapist got him ankle braces to stabilize his feet, and by age three we shifted him from physical therapy to balance (vestibular) therapy. He had one surgery just before he turned two, to finally repair what had become a pretty severe double hernia. But that was it. None of his residual birth issues became a disabling condition. In fact, when Dan and I attended our first parent-teacher conference at his pre-school when he was four, we braced ourselves to learn that he might be delayed cognitively. But when the teacher said he was "above average," we couldn't believe our ears. My eyes were visibly stunned. Then I cried, and the teacher had no idea why. We explained. "Danny had quite the birth history, and we were sure that he'd be a little behind, just as he has been with his gross motor development." She was surprised to learn this, and hadn't even noticed his gross motor delays. *Wow, Danny is above average?!* We only told family, because they would understand. We were in the clear.

When we brought Danny home from the hospital to finally live with us, we couldn't know how it would turn out or if there would ever be such a moment. When Danny was two, he knocked a drill off of a table that fell directly into (and through) his foot. The ER doctor, after seeing the X-ray that indicated that the drill missed his bones, said, "He is fortunate in his misfortune." He didn't know just how true those words rang.

In this journey of intense highs and lows, I had developed a sense for what I could control and what I couldn't. Three times Danny's news had turned to threats of death: the in-utero challenges, the preemie risks, and then the meningitis. We had just spent the last four months on a consistent pattern of highs and lows, and I had eventually relaxed into them. Not only had I learned to realize when I had no control, but I also learned to think, act, and feel like I had no control. Though I had clearly learned these lessons — that unexpected bad things just happen and that there are limits to what I can control — I still had yet to learn all the contexts of my life where those lessons would apply. The following years would provide the opportunity to make those connections.

At Pearl Harbor, three years earlier, I had had the overwhelming feeling of guilt for having held any feelings of pride or connection to the experience of death. Sure, the grief I felt had been my own, but I had watched others deal with the news of their own death and felt special to have been a spectator. This time, though, I felt a crossing over. I did not face my *own* mortality, but with my son's fetal and infant level of consciousness, I faced his mortality more than he did. Friends and family gave *me* the looks of unspoken discomfort. I have heard from those who would know that losing a child is the worst grief that a person can experience, that a large piece of yourself dies with the child. That's what I had faced. I *was* dying, a large part of me had teetered right there in the balance.

While we were in the clear with Danny's health, my tenure application was not so fortunate. Due to my limited number of publications, I was denied tenure and given a year to find a new position. This spelled the end of our time in Hawai'i, and I found myself uncertain about my next step. Our decision over what to do next was, in part, decided for us when Dan was hired at a small college in Virginia, not far from my hometown. We were leaving Hawai'i, but no matter how far away we moved, one of my most important relationships there forever changed my connection with death.

Chapter 19

Grace

After my kids were born and I continued to figure out my family routine and professional life, my friend, Grace, continued to be a solid constant in my life. Grace was a colleague, neighbor, and friend. I met Grace when she was hired in August 2008, just six months after Rebecca died and a few months after Peyton was born. Grace had a bright smile, with smooth high cheek bones and shoulder-length black hair. She was happy and quirky with a quick raucous laugh, and I liked her. We easily became fast friends.

Grace was originally from Taiwan, although she hadn't lived there in eighteen years — for just as many years since I had left my home state of Virginia. Grace was Buddhist. I'd known other Buddhists, but none as devout as Grace was. Many were Buddhist in name and ritual, whereas Grace studied Buddha's history, philosophy, and writings. She took online courses on meditation, owned few possessions, and ate a vegetarian diet. We were close in age — Grace was five years older.

I invited Grace to my writing group, neighborhood walks, and potluck parties. She introduced me to homemade soymilk and thousand-year-old eggs (cracked eggs hard-boiled in tea). Eventually we settled into a routine every Friday and met for an early morning ocean swim. We'd swim independently for 30 minutes, then sit on the beach together, people-watch, and share breakfast. She'd bring a fun new tropical fruit to try or her homemade bread, and I'd just bring boring granola bars or fruit. We'd marvel at this glorious place that we were both lucky to call home. We loved our Friday morning routine and were pretty protective of keeping the standing date. My kids loved their Auntie Grace. She enjoyed making faces at them and playing peek-a-boo, and look-what-I-can-do. Grace took a pass on our chaotic kid-friendly family parties, but we were pleased to call each other family friends.

Our offices were next door to each other, so it was easy to rely on each other for professional and even personal advice. In early May 2011, I confided in Grace when I received the news that I lost my contract. No tenure for me. I had hoped that it would somehow be possible to support my young family and Dan's dissertation writing and still be able to produce as much as was expected of me. Later when I job searched in Virginia, a department chair at a research institution shared how impressed she was that I had published as much as I had with two infants. But it wasn't enough for my Hawai'i institution. My fears and "what ifs" from my long walk into the Manoa Valley all came flooding back. Our dream of living in Hawai'i necessarily came to an end as did my professional identity. And Grace had been there for me through those painful moments.

My husband's new job would be moving us away from Hawai'i in a matter of months, and back to my home state of Virginia. After all of Danny's complications, moving back closer to home seemed the best support we would all need. Since I hadn't lived in my home state for 18 years, it was a big deal to leave paradise and return to the vaguely familiar.

Though I wouldn't move until July that year, I began my good-bye with Grace in May because she was planning to spend some extended summer time in her home city of Taipei visiting her family. She hadn't visited her home for more than a couple of weeks at a time since moving to the US nearly 20 years earlier. This trip would be her longest visit to her hometown since she'd moved away. Before she'd return back to Hawai'i in August, I would have already moved to Virginia. We were both headed toward immersions into our familiar but distant pasts – me to Virginia and Grace to Taipei – and we knew that our friendship would take a turn toward rare contacts.

With a week to go until our good-bye, Grace poked her head into my office. "Do you have a moment to talk?"

"Well, I want to get this done," motioning to some pressing work I had on my desk. "After that?"

"Yes, sure. It is important, but not urgent. Definitely come by when you can."

My interest was piqued. *What could it be? Did she get news from home? Was it related to work?* I rushed what I was doing towards a good stopping point rather than waiting until I was done. I went to her office and she wasn't there. I took a seat and waited. She had posters on her wall of past professional conferences and pictures of colleagues she had known through the years.

She returned from the restroom, and smiled to see me there. She turned to close the door for privacy; this was serious. She sat down across from me and pulled her chair close. She leaned in toward me and smiled again.

"I have breast cancer." She checked my face to make sure I was okay.

"Oh Grace, I'm so sorry." *Again?! Shit. I'm going to lose another friend.* I kept my poise. "I…I'm so sorry. That's not good at all. I don't know what else to say. I'm so sorry." We studied each other's faces in quiet tension to see how we each felt. "Um, how long have you known?"

"I found out this morning. I had my regular mammogram last week, and they left a message earlier this week. I finally talked to someone today." Still smiling, and yet very serious.

"You found out on the phone?!"

"Yes, but it was well done, I thought. The doctor was insistent on being the one to tell me — not a message and not an assistant. So even though we swapped voicemails a couple times, it was he who told me. And he wants me to come in as soon as I can, and he didn't want me to wonder why."

"That makes sense. So, wow, this is fresh information for you."

"Oh yes. My mind has been racing."

"Who else have you told?"

"I told Ji Yeon." Ji Yeon was one of our writing group buddies. "She knew that I had the appointment last week. She knew that I needed to return the call from the doctor's office. I put it off because I didn't think much of it. But she insisted and followed up with me. She was right. When the doctor himself calls, it's serious. But other than she, no one. I *just* found out."

"So your family doesn't know. Wait?! When are you supposed to leave for Taiwan?"

"A week from today." She grinned hard with furrowed brow.

"And stay for the entire two months? You can't do that."

"I know. Well maybe I can. Maybe I can get treatments there."

"What about health insurance?"

"Every citizen there has access to comprehensive healthcare; and I'm still a citizen. I have a green card here."

"Wow, that's amazing. So what kind of treatment are they recommending?"

"Kelly, I just found out a couple hours ago. All I know is that I have cancer."

"Right, sorry."

"They scheduled an appointment for me tomorrow for a surgeon's consultation. I wanted to tell you about this quickly, because, well, I'd like for you to come with me."

I was touched. "Absolutely. When?"

"Tomorrow at 11a.m. I want you to pay attention and be an extra set of ears. I fear I'll get overwhelmed, and zone out. I'll miss important information, and forget to ask my questions. And, you know, just moral support."

"Right. That's a great idea." My experience with my son's health just one year earlier left me feeling confident in my ability to sort through medical information.

"So let's talk about the questions you have, and I'll write them down." I considered it my job to keep track of them and to make sure they all got answered.

"I want to know what stage I am in. Everything I read in terms of prognosis depends on what stage I am. I want to know why they are having me meet with a surgeon and not an oncologist."

"Oh, right, I wonder if that means something. Why skip the oncologist?"

"Right, and I need to make a decision about my flight as soon as I can."

"So what would you need to know in order to make a good decision?"

"I'll need to know what treatments they suggest, if they can wait and how long, and if I can start them under someone else's care."

"Right. What if they insist that you stay? Could you? Would you?"

"I think I'll still go, but I might need to come back sooner. And, well, there's another issue."

"What?"

"You know when you're personally faced with a situation it's much different than observing it from the outside looking in."

"Of course, you must be overwhelmed beyond ways I can imagine."

"Yes, well, as a Buddhist, I've often thought that the Western 'cut 'n kill' approach to cancer is not what I'd want to do."

"Oh…OH, so you're wondering if you'll even want to do what they suggest?"

"Right. But now that I have cancer, I'm not so quick to decide that. I'm feeling scared enough, desperate enough, that I wonder if I should go the Western way."

"I had no idea that there were other ways to treat cancer. What other choice do you have? What are the alternatives? What does Traditional Chinese Medicine do with cancer?"

"There are other ways, healing the whole self – body, mind, and heart – all as one. I am really faced with what I truly believe, and my life is on the line."

"And you don't really have the luxury of time to sort this out."

"Right."

This sounded familiar to me. I've read critiques of the US healthcare system, with specialists who focus on too narrow of an aspect of anyone's health, forgetting that the human body is a mass of interconnected systems. I've read Eastern perspectives of development that critique Descartes for his vision of bodies, minds, and souls as separate things when they should not be distinguished lest the separation destroy us. At this moment, I envisioned that Traditional Chinese Medicine (TCM) had holistic medications, maybe even herbal remedies, that the West probably judged negatively. I had no idea that even my fanciful vision of Eastern medicine was still so deeply rooted in the West.

The next day, my list in hand, we drove to the appointment in town. The staff at the doctor's office appreciated our position. They greeted Grace with deferential care but not pity. At the reception desk, waiting area, and doctor's exam room, they responded quickly, never leaving us anywhere for long periods of time to wait. They offered water to us both. They must figure, if you're going to go out with cancer, you might as well have a cup of water while we chat about it.

The surgeon was kind and honest. He asked Grace how she had been feeling emotionally. Then he asked how she felt health-wise.

"You know, I'm not sure," she responded. "I think I know where the cancer might be. Ever since I heard the news, I think I feel ill, but then I think that I didn't think that before the news, so how much of this is real?"

"That actually makes a lot of sense, and we can talk more about that, but first I want to ask where you think it is."

"Right here," as she slowly pointed directly at the center of her left nipple.

"Exactly." He showed Grace the images from her mammogram. "Here you can see the size of the mass; the cancer is this smooth black area here," he said, pointing to a clearly defined almond-shaped mass. "We would call this stage one. Your lymph nodes, here, are clear. So, this is actually relatively good news. We can get this."

"But the five-year survival rates are still around 70% for stage one for my age group."

"Right, but that's changing every day, and obviously those rates are at least five years old. Advancements in breast cancer research are making big differences."

"What are you recommending?"

"We have a pretty good idea of the rate of growth because your last mammogram a year ago was clear, and this is stage one now. Another thing I consider is your age. The younger you are, and at 44, I consider you towards the young side, the more fatal breast cancer can be. But, also the younger you are, you can handle more aggressive treatments. You have some choices here.

First, I say we need to schedule your surgery for as early as next week. You have some surgery options — lumpectomy or mastectomy." He reviewed the pros and cons of each with glossy brochures to highlight the differences.

Grace seemed quick to decide. "Mastectomy looks like the way to go. Why go halfway when there are more benefits to going all the way. I don't need that breast."

I was impressed. She sounded brave. And she seemed to be warming to the idea of cutting the cancer.

Then her face changed, "But, still, it's my body."

Right, there it is. That's the real truth. This is Grace's body.

"Well, you can take these brochures and take some time to decide. Then I think we follow up the surgery with at least radiation. I would also recommend chemotherapy just to be sure. You are young enough to handle it, but old enough that it will be very tough on your body. But that can be up to you. It's a quality-of-life decision."

I knew what was on Grace's mind, so I asked, "Isn't it *all* up to her?"

"Well, right, but if survival is your goal your choices are limited."

How do I carefully word this without offending the surgeon? Without taking Grace's voice? "Surely you've heard of folks who refuse the cut and kill approach." I made a face as if to say, but that's not us of course. "What is your response to those folks?" I wanted Grace to hear his answer.

"I think the evidence stands for itself. The most successful approach is what I'm recommending to you here. Nothing else has a better survival rate. Nothing. If there was a non-surgery natural approach that worked, we'd be doing that." As a PhD, who values research, I wondered if the surgeon's message struck a chord with Grace. It seemed pretty powerful to me.

I'd hoped that Grace would explain her travel plans. I didn't want to continue to speak for her, but she was quiet.

"Grace has airplane tickets to go to Taipei next week. Can the surgery and treatment wait? And how long?" I hope that the physician didn't think that I had my priorities screwed up.

"Uhh, that's a hard one. Only the cancer knows how fast it's going to progress. I'd say she should get started in no more than a couple weeks."

"So, Grace, you could go home for a week and then come back to get started." She looked at me as if to say, *Um, no.*

I worried that I was speaking too much, but trusted that that's why she wanted me to come. To get her questions asked. "Grace's intentions were to stay in Taiwan all summer. Could she get treatment there?"

"I suppose. We can share our images and test results. But the treatment will likely require supervised care for longer than just the summer. I could pick it up from there once she returns, but we'd all need to be on the same page. It could be a challenge. Medicine there is quite different. I'd recommend that you keep consistent care somewhere. Or I could have my office identify a practice in Taipei that would give you consistent care."

"We were curious why we're meeting with you as Grace's first point of contact. No offense, but of course the surgeon is going to suggest surgery. Shouldn't we get the opinion of an oncologist?"

"You're welcome to get another opinion, and I can set you up with one if you like. You can also find your own. Our rationale is that time is of the essence, and surgery is the obvious first step to getting cancer out of the body. If you get another opinion, do that by the end of this week."

That's not really what we had in mind.

As we walked out, Grace gathered her brochures about surgery options and chemo treatments. She turned down the doctor's offer to provide names for secondary opinions. She did not make an appointment for a surgery, but left promising that she'd call back tomorrow with her decision about how to move forward. As we left, I thought Grace was on board for the treatments, but just struggling to figure out what to do about her travel arrangements. I was wrong.

Our conversation in the car on our way back to work was about processing the current situation, not about making decisions. "Wow, that's a lot to think about…There are some big decisions to make…Who do you want to talk to about the decision?…Have you told your mom yet?…Your sister?" I didn't want to pressure her with my burning question, *What will you decide?* It was too soon.

The next day I asked Grace if she'd called back the surgeon's office yet. She hadn't. I was curious about her decision, but it seemed that maybe she didn't have one yet.

When two days had passed, my curiosity couldn't be contained any longer. The next time I saw Grace in the office, I asked, "So are you headed to Taipei in a few days or what?"

"Yes. Yes I am."

"Annnd...? When will you return?"

"I'm going to figure it out there. I need to discuss it with people there — my family and some specialists."

"Does your mom know yet?"

"Yes."

"How'd she take it?"

"She just wants me to come home. This was already going to be a weird trip to live with my mother for two months. Now this. Everything has changed."

"She'll be so glad to see you."

"She will."

"Do you need a ride to the airport?" *And will it be the last time I ever see you?*

"Yes, actually, that would be great. And I hope I can give you my car keys. I want you to take care of my car and drive it about once a week to keep it running."

"Sure, I can do that. My pleasure."

Grace left for Taiwan and wasn't gone long before she called to let me know that she had decided to take a full-year medical absence from work. She wasn't coming back home to Honolulu for a year. Her own leave time would only get her so far, so her department chair offered to help coordinate an effort to collect donated sick days through the university's human resources office. I was impressed. She'd be gone a whole year.

"Did you find what you were looking for in a doctor there?"

"Um, yes, kind of. Not exactly a medical doctor, but exactly what I was looking for. I have some pills I take daily, a mountain I climb every morning, and there's a long list of intensive personal work that I need to do. It will take all year."

"I'm glad that worked out." But I felt like she wasn't telling me everything. *What kind of intensive work? Why does it take all year? What's in those pills?*

I helped her to sell her car, to release her apartment, and to move her out of it. I missed her. Big things were happening in her life, and I'd only get to be on the periphery. I wouldn't know or understand what was going on. It would be too hard to have these conversations long distance. Cancer conversations are best had in person. And I knew I was bad at having phone conversations. I feared losing Grace like I lost Miriam and Rebecca, no good-byes–just an email message from a stranger someday.

Chapter 20

Taiwan

In July 2011, my family made our big move from Hawai'i to central Virginia. I continued to teach online for the University of Hawai'i one more year, so I had unprecedented income and time available to me. I had enough frequent-flyer miles from living in Hawai'i for four years to go to Taiwan for just $90. Grace also had unprecedented time and income — a full year off with sick leave pay. It was a perfect opportunity to get together. Besides, I wanted to truly know how Grace was doing, to be there for her, but via distance it was difficult to establish that kind of connection. I booked a trip for my spring break to Taiwan in March 2012.

The fall before my trip, my beloved grandmother's health deteriorated quickly. She had surgery to fix an internal bleeding situation; she never really recovered. She moved from independent living to assisted living to nursing care within a few months. I traveled to visit her in Indiana to ensure she could see Peyton again for the second time and meet Danny for the first time. She saw herself in Danny, his struggle for survival and health. That had been her birth story, too. The story goes that she was six months old and just five pounds, not taking to milk. It was mashed peas that saved her. She loved Danny before she'd even met him. Their meeting seemed like the release, the permission she needed to let go and die. In my imagination, she had held on to meet her most recent great-grandchild, and now it was done. I held her smooth face in my hand and kissed her cheeks. I held her hand. We sat and tried to talk, but she had trouble hearing. I felt like I was yelling at her as I tried to say anything, so we just watched the young cousins playing around us while I held on tightly to her hand and would occasionally hug her. She wanted to talk, and I couldn't. I just wanted to hold onto her as long as I could before I needed to head back to my life in Virginia.

Once when I was in the fifth grade during a visit with my grandparents, I woke to an ambulance siren in their neighborhood. It suddenly occurred to me that my grandparents would one day die. I sat up in bed crying as my grandmother comforted me. "Dying is a natural part of life," she explained. When I was in college and my grandfather, her husband, passed, she took it all in stride. She supported the mourning of the family and leaned in hard to her own growth and development afterward. I had always thought of her as a model for how to bravely face death.

When it was her turn, she was ready. Surviving had become hard work for her, and she was tired of it. She was ready to go, but she would have to wait. Her days were spent mostly sleeping and wondering why she woke up each day. She'd say, "Dying is not for the weak" with a disgruntled laugh. In her last months, she was starting to forget that her family loved her and that they were visiting her regularly. She felt alone, ill, and weak. She was upset that her children didn't visit her. They did, she just didn't remember. She felt alone, but she wasn't.

Through that November, Grandma lost her confidence in death. Fear set in. As she regretted waking each day, she grew frustrated at God. She was not grateful for life, at least not life in those last days. She felt sinful for being impatient to go. She worried that God knew her heart and would be disappointed in her. She wept with exhaustion. Could God forgive her? Just too much for my sweet grandmother to take.

As Grandma's 93rd birthday approached, November 25, my mother became certain that she wouldn't live to see it. I told Mom then, "No, she'll see her birthday. She'll die on *my* birthday–that's just what happens." And that's exactly what happened.

A few months after my grandmother's death, I spent ten days with Grace in Taiwan where she showed off her country, family, religion, and personal health to me. She was my own personal tour guide and translator. We spent half the week in the sky-scraping urban center of Taipei. By day we visited public landmarks like the National Palace Museum, Chiang Kai-Shek Memorial Hall, Sun Yat-sen Memorial Hall, and Taipei 101 — previously the tallest building in the world. We punctuated each evening with a visit to one of Grace's favorite restaurants which all featured vegetarian goodies of unusual – to me – colors, smells, textures, and flavors. The famous Shilin Night Market was among my most memorable meals there. Vibrant neon signs overhead guided us through the market. We walked through packed vendors selling shiny red whole fish, inverted skinned ducks, stinky tofu, corncob on a stick, fresh-squeezed-on-the-spot orange juice, and plenty of foods I could not identify. We snacked on veggie dumplings and deep-fried tofu on sticks as we wove through colorful displays of tourist gear, magic tricks, and snake charmers. The second half of the trip we traveled by fast-train along the eastern perimeter of the island south through the lush green tropical and mountainous countryside into smaller cities like Hualien and Taitung. We walked the beach, soaked in a natural hot spring, made jade necklaces, visited Taroko Gorge, and toured a nature history museum where Grace's uncle once worked.

Taiwan was gorgeous and felt familiar. The mountains toward the center of the island and the numerous ocean views lined with swaying palm trees easily reminded me of Hawai'i. The air in Taiwan was similarly humid with frequent misty rains, but the temperatures were cooler.

One evening in Taipei, after a full day of exploring Shilin Market, we entered Longshan Temple. I learned that Longshan is a functioning Buddhist and Taoist temple, built in 1738 by Chinese settlers from Fujian. To me, the temple appeared to pop up out of the middle of the sidewalk on a street corner, majestic with a red glazed roof. I felt too awkward to walk in; I didn't want to interrupt or gawk at people as they practiced their religion. I assumed in my Western mind that it would be a service or some sort of organized program. Through crowds of tourists and worshipers, Grace led me inside through a small hidden entryway, but I was nervous about following. With reddish brown hair and no hat or hood, I could not sneak in. I would be noticed. I didn't know the religion; I wouldn't know what I was seeing. I worried that my entry would be disrespectful. Would I be perceived as a gawker, as someone who wouldn't be welcome?

"Are people worshipping now?"

"Yes."

"I can't go in there, Grace. I don't want to intrude."

"It's okay. All of these people are tourists."

"But aren't they worshipping tourists?"

"Yes, probably most of them, but it's okay. You'll blend in."

How is that even possible? But she was right. No one even looked at me; they were busy with their offerings and rituals. Too devout to notice me, it seemed.

The woodwork of the temple was ornate, with so many golden details that it didn't appear wooden at all. And yet it was masterfully crafted with large twisting columns carved out of entire trees. No glue, metal screws, or nails were used to assemble the decor. The artistry seemed grand and yet the space felt intimate. From the outside it appeared to be one building, but inside revealed a tight campus of open pavilions. There were no doors — just a twisting path of open archways. Once inside, you could look up and see the sky. Atop the roof, silhouetted against the light blue sky, sat colorfully glazed blue dragons with red features breathing fire at each other.

Although few people spoke, the air was full of the sounds of busyness — feet shuffling, whispers, and soft hypnotic chanting. I had expected to see a service that we would interrupt, but there was no service, no program.

Straight ahead Grace pointed out several tables piled high with flowers and fruits.

"Is there an event? We should leave. It looks like they're setting up for a reception?"

"No, no. It's an offering table."

"But someone is taking stuff from it."

"Yeah, it's funny. They believe it's an offering to the deities, but who will receive it? No one. So some will come, lay down an offering while they are here, then take it back when they leave."

To my left, a group of people seemed engaged as they faced an altar. They held thin red carved flat sticks roughly the size of incense sticks, each person holding two. They seemed to be praying, but not aloud, just murmuring to themselves. Several put their sticks together and held the lower tips to their forehead while pointing the other ends toward the shrine, appearing like earnest unicorns. Others in this same group did not have the prayer sticks. They rubbed two red crescent-shaped blocks in their hands and dropped them to the floor, then picked them up again, repeating the process.

"This is a ritual to ask questions of the gods. They get the fortune sticks from that canister over there. Then they think and meditate clearly on the question for some time as they face the altar. Their minds can't shift or the gods won't be able to answer. The sticks themselves indicate a code that is associated with their fortune, which they receive on a slip of paper over there. They return their sticks to the cylinder. Then they drop the crescent blocks, or *jiaobei*, to find the answer. It depends on how they land as to what the answer is. One of the positions means try again, so they do that often."

"It's quite a sight, isn't it?" I heard from behind.

I turned when a man's voice behind me caught my attention. He sat on a bench along the wall. "I could sit here for hours and watch this. So much purpose and meaning to these activities within these walls." He was an older white man. I chatted with him for a bit. He was observing the people in the temple. Maybe studying them. He was the gawker that I feared I was. I projected my fears about my own motivations onto him. In hindsight, perhaps he was trying to tell me something valuable, something about life and purpose and humanity, but I wasn't ready to hear. Instead, I judged him in my thoughts and then followed Grace to the next section.

More ornate structures were surrounded by barred cages to protect the artistry from the masses. Grace told me the story of this one and that one. We found our way to the back of the temple, where several shrines representing Chinese folk-gods were lined up along the wall. Each was an ornate golden personification surrounded by vibrant décor — all protected by red painted gates.

Pointing to the first one, Grace said, "This is the god for fortune. People down on their financial luck pray to this one." A man raised his head and made intense eye contact with the idol and shook incense at it.

"This one is for wishing for a mate, to find true love. And on the other side of that one is another for wishing for a baby; many infertile couples come here." I saw a man and woman there with their child. I imagined that having a second child was proving difficult for them. Or maybe they were sending up thanks for the child they had successfully wished for.

"This one is Buddha, a Chinese version. And this one over here is for health."

"Are all of these Buddhist gods?"

"Some, sort of. Most are folk deities."

"Do you need to pay your respects here? Should I walk over there to give you some privacy?"

"Oh no. No, this isn't the kind of Buddhism that I observe. Actually, this isn't really Buddhism. This is just ancient ritual that somehow got mixed up in Buddhism. This has nothing to do with the teachings of Buddha. Many of them think it does." She motioned to the incense shakers.

This sounded familiar. Some Christians say this of other Christians — that their rituals are not based on Jesus's teachings. Jehovah's Witnesses say this particularly about Catholic and Protestant traditions. This is how I made sense of Grace's comments.

"Did you ever do this? Or do your family members do this? Are you the one who broke away?"

"My family never really did this. But my interest in Buddha was more or less just me. My sister has become more interested. I became very interested in Buddha in college. I've read his writings which is not common. A smaller portion of Buddhists study the teachings."

"What drew you to it?"

She smiled, "What a remarkable human! He was so profound and enlightened so long ago, and humanity is still searching for these answers. But, the answers have been available for so long."

"When was Buddha's lifetime?"

"He lived in the region of Nepal and India over 2,500 years ago."

The haze from the incense set into my vision. The meditation sounds settled past my ears and into my forehead as my whole face relaxed. In this dream-like state, Grace told me the story of Buddha's enlightenment. I could imagine no better way to hear the story of Prince Siddhartha Gautama's six-year search for enlightenment. Early on, he noticed that suffering is an unavoidable part of all human life. At minimum we all have the capacity to get sick and grow old, and we all die. I was hearing this all for the first time, so the lessons would take time to sink in and connect to my own experiences with death. The next day Grace offered me a chance to put some of my new learnings into practice.

The next Saturday was a memorable day. I was one of more than 100 attendees at a 12-kilometer walking silent meditative retreat for beginning meditators. The retreat was run through a Buddhist organization called the Dharma Drum, an organization to which Grace belonged. Grace had arranged in advance with the organizers that she would be my interpreter. She had been a participant at this event six months before and found it valuable, and she wanted to share the experience with me.

We knew in advance that it would be a chilly (in the 50s F) and wet day, so I wore the warmest clothes that I brought, a rain jacket, and walking shoes. We took a city train to the last stop on one of the train lines, and we met the group at a nearby park. I didn't know what to expect and didn't consider in advance if I should behave any differently than I usually would. Grace immediately saw volunteers for the event and lifted her praying hands to them, shaking them at her forehead, and saying some sort of greeting as she approached. *Should I have made praying hands? Should I have bowed? Oh, right, bowing! I should have bowed.* But the moment passed. It was too late.

This was a complete cultural immersion day for me. I was the only non-Taiwanese person at the event, the only one using a translator, not to mention the only one who didn't have black hair. I imagine I may have also been the only non-Buddhist. I stood out.

The leader for the day was a Buddhist nun. She had a shaven head with a black ski cap and a conical "Chinese farmer's hat" over it. She wore a gray smock, socks pulled up to what looked like long-johns, and simple sandals over the socks. She had a delightful smile that lit up everyone's mood. Grace walked directly to her and, I assumed, introduced me to her. She bowed (again, I forgot to bow) then made a gesture with her hand that indicated to me that she wanted to shake my hand. *Oh*, I thought, *she wants to meet me where I am and shake my hand.* So I put my hand right out there, and...nope, she was motioning where we needed to go. She saw my hand and laughed and bowed again. So I bowed, and laughed at myself. *Silly American, BOW!* The nun asked Grace to convey a story to me about an elderly enlightened man who, with a group, hiked up the many stairs to the very tall St. Peter's Basilica lookout deck in Rome. After he reached the top he was the only person who was not tired. The others asked him why he was not tired. He explained that he viewed every step as if it were the only step, disregarding any consideration of the steps behind him or the steps before him. Just this one. The nun encouraged me to treat the hike today in a similar way. "Twelve kilometers may seem like a lot, but if you keep your focus on each step then your energy will remain with you to the end." *That's a nice message.* I wasn't concerned at all about hiking. *Isn't twelve kilometers just seven miles, right? No big deal.* If it was a run, I'd be thinking more about it, but a walk, *it's just walking right? I can walk. No problem.*

We were up on a mountain walking along a path through the woods revealing occasional views of the city. We were 100 hikers walking in single file, all of us in matching disposable yellow plastic raincoats. I'm sure we were a sight to behold. We were instructed to be silent the entire walk, and to concentrate on our present, on being aware, but not thinking. I really struggled with that. *How is awareness different from thinking? How can I turn one off and leave the other on?*

"You will know the answer to your question when you no longer have the question." This was Grace's advice to me. She explained, "It sounds silly at first, but it's true ...and it's true about every question." She laughed her hearty laugh. I wanted to laugh with her, but the tone of the day allowed me to see that she was serious so her message began to sink in. Her comment stuck with me in this moment, but it would be years before I understood how broadly her advice would apply. The deeper message was this: Do not become anxious about not knowing answers. Do not think your way through this. Pivot attention away from "figuring it out," away from solutions and toward the question itself. Allow the question to just sit. Marvel at the question. Observe the question. Ask, "How do I relate to this question?" Do this with quiet time and it's called "meditating on a question." And one day, when you no longer have the question, you will know that somehow you have found an answer.

As I've practiced this strategy of meditating on questions over the years, I've come to a realization. Often the answers to my burning questions are already inside me, deep inside me among the recesses of my past experiences and life lessons. Many of my burning life questions are just bad questions — questions that represent faulty assumptions that my conscious brain is holding onto. Meditating on the question allows me time and space to open up my awareness to realize that either I already know the answer, or the question was a bad question and it disappears. *Why did an unfair thing just happen?! ... Because life is not fair, but you already knew that. Why are bad things happening to me? ... Because you are human, and you already knew that, too.*

There was much more going on for me this day in the mountains overlooking Taipei than just meditation training — I was completely immersed, and much was unfamiliar. We ate our lunch with meditative instruction. I learned how to eat with awareness. I had no idea what I was eating at lunch. It was not difficult to eat with awareness as every bite was a new experience. I put things in my mouth that looked awful but tasted great, and something that looked great but tasted awful after taking a big bite of it. We were instructed to clean our plates, so I did — with a little help from Grace.

After lunch, our guides instructed us to line up in single file rows to face the nun who was standing under the overhang of a retreat building tucked into the woods. Grace turned to me, "This exercise helped me to understand my cancer. This was a big moment for me. But I want you to experience this on your own first before I tell you what it meant to me. Definitely give it your best."

As the nun spoke, Grace translated her story to me as quietly as she could. She told us the story of a cultivator (someone striving for enlightenment) who was given a test of his awareness by his king. He was told to carry a small bowl of oil to the next kingdom through the woods along a ridge. He was told that if he spilled just one drop of oil he would be executed. The king provided soldier escorts to watch him — and to taunt and distract him. But the cultivator was successful. He was aware of his surroundings, because he needed that awareness to navigate the way, but he did not think about his surroundings, because his attention would have been taken away from his oil bowl.

To exercise our awareness over our thinking, we were going to carry out a similar mission. The nun encouraged us to give it the same level of seriousness, as if our lives were at stake. We were each given a small bowl of water filled to the top and instructed to walk a quarter-mile loop that included a downhill slope, then uphill walking over large stones, then stairs with six steps, then along a flat road. As I waited to get my water bowl, I saw the people before me begin their course. People were no longer walking in a single file line. Some were quicker than others and could pass people. Others were slow and still spilled a lot. The nun spoke into her microphone, "Be one with the bowl. The bowl is you. You are not an adversary with the bowl." I didn't know what that meant for me. I walked with my usual gait but in super slow motion. I was careful where I put my foot. I was very aware of shifting my weight from one foot to the other, because this was when I was more apt to lose water. Mid-way through the course, I tried a step-together-step gait that provided me more stability. I did feel at one with my bowl and passed others. But as soon as I was aware that I was doing this, I spilled. *Slow down. Stop thinking.*

I was reminded of the phenomenon that when you think too hard about walking upstairs you trip yourself up. As soon as you don't think about it, you can run up the stairs with ease. Same with water bowls. *Don't think and it's easy. Think and I spill. Ah, I've GOT IT! Finally. I understand what it means to not think, and how harmony and peace can be the result. It is a metaphor that I can think back to when I need help in understanding. The bowl. Think about the bowl. Be one with the bowl.* But my inability to differentiate between my own awareness versus thinking meant that I'd cruise the course one minute, then spill the next, having no idea what I had done differently to make that occur. *I'm fighting it, trying to control it. Relax. How is this done?* I was only beginning to understand.

Later, we took an optional restroom break on a mountain-top with a view of the wooded area we had just hiked up. The restrooms were located in a nearly ruined, yet ornate building with boarded-up windows and large chunks of red and blue paint flaking off the borders, and dragons sitting atop the roof with heads, tails, or wings knocked off. I had never seen such a scene before, and yet I was physically standing in it. I quietly made eye contact with Grace and mouthed, "I have so many questions."

"Ask," she whispered bravely.

"Well, not now, right?" I whispered back with hesitation. "Don't we need to stay silent?"

"Go ahead and ask discreetly. That should be fine."

"Well, first, what is this place? Is this an abandoned Buddhist temple?"

"Yes."

"There's a swastika on it. I know it means something in indigenous American spirituality, but I didn't know it's connected to Buddhists?"

"It pre-dates Buddha." *Whoa.* I had no idea. "What else?"

"I can't stop thinking."

"I know."

"Is it possible?"

"Yes."

"But how?"

She smiled, "You will know the answer when you no longer have the question."

I smiled, too, then smirked, "That doesn't help."

"What did you think of the water bowl?"

"That was difficult. Just when I thought I understood it, I'd think too much and lose it. But, I think I was beginning to get it." I told her my analogy of running upstairs, and she agreed that was a good example.

"But, Grace, you were going to tell me your experience with the water bowl. You were able to do it, weren't you?"

"Not at first. I was spilling." Grace took a deep breath. "The nun kept repeating over and over, 'Be one with the bowl; it is not your adversary.' Just as I hit my stride and moved with the bowl spill-free — it clicked. The bowl is my cancer. Be one with the cancer. It is a part of me; don't fight it. Embrace it. Love it. It *is* me. I continued the course with awareness and love for this bowl, no spills. I was elated. I knew what I had to do. Be one with the cancer."

"That is deep, Grace."

"It is."

It was beautiful, and it served as a pathway to my own understanding of Grace's approach to her cancer and life. *Much later*, this would be a pathway I'd eventually adopt for myself. My struggle with the demands of motherhood, my job loss, and the deaths of so many peers were all parts of me that I could learn to love with compassion.

Grace explained, "This cancer has given me a beautiful struggle. I'm so grateful for this opportunity to be genuine, discover, and forgive. I wouldn't be experiencing this without the cancer."

Over the course of my visit, in subtle doses, I would understand what Grace meant by the beautiful struggle. I managed to ask the burning questions that I had left in Hawai'i nearly a year ago: *How are you treating your cancer? What is in those pills? Why does it take a year? What exactly does it mean to have a TCM approach to cancer? How are you feeling? Is it working for you?* The answers unfolded over several days.

First, Grace explained that before I arrived in Taipei, her daily routine consisted of early morning qi-gong exercises, followed by a mountain hike on the periphery of the city where she could get a view of a quaint neighborhood below. Occasionally, she'd even head down to that area and have a light breakfast before returning up and over the mountain back home. But since I was in town, we'd be hiking enough with sightseeing. She did continue with qi-gong every day. She'd wake up at 5 a.m. every day, and find a private place to practice the exercises. From what I could tell, qi-gong involved meditative, deliberate, and repetitive movements that encouraged awareness of the self. She would swing her arms, repeatedly and pay attention to the details of the motion, feeling the energy and being present — becoming one with the motion, not fighting it, nor forcing it. Then she'd twist her body in a different motion and meditate through that. Following the exercises, she needed one hour of rest, as this was part of the practice and the reason the exercises started so early in the morning. She explained that she'd appreciate quiet from me as well. No problem! I was thrilled to oblige. I love lounging in my bed after I wake up — an hour was fantastic.

Grace was no longer taking any pills. They were homeopathic anyway, nothing much more than vitamins. Grace explained that the approach she's following is healing her entire body, so yes, this would take time. She had read a book called *The Secret to Healing Cancer: A Chinese Psychiatrist and Family Doctor Presents His Amazing Method for Curing Cancer through Psychological and Spiritual Growth* by Dr. Hsu Tien-Sheng. Grace knew this was the approach she wanted to take, and I discovered that the approach is not TCM or Buddhism at all, rather its spiritual origins are based in new age mystics. She found professional help to follow the method from the author himself, who was located right in Taipei at the Holistic Clinic. She explained that this approach calls cancer a dis-ease rather than a disease. Cancer is viewed as a symptom of an unhealthy body, and not the cause. Cancer grows in sick bodies, so to make the cancer heal, make the body healthy. Dr. Hsu's clinic helped her to explore all the unhealthy relationships she's ever had, and do the hard work to heal those relationships. Past boyfriends came up. So she searched them down and talked to them about what had happened and apologized for her role in any negative outcomes. The biggest healing had to be done with her mother, with whom she was now living. She told me how her perspective on her relationship with her mother had changed, and the strategies that she learned from her healer. Grace was doing the hard work that others might avoid.

According to Hsu, the three basic principles of health and healing are: 1) we are naturally healthy, 2) our bodies can heal themselves, and 3) the physical body is a reflection of the mind. Grace explained, "If we believe in these three principles, then we can start the journey of healing." On one hand, this made sense to me. Shannon's story with her father helped me to see that unhealed psychological pain would manifest somehow – dreams, hurting others – so it seemed likely that physical disease could be another manifestation. On the other hand, I wondered about Nick, Miriam, and Rebecca — if they had unhealed psychological pain that I didn't know about. Or maybe some cancers were dis-ease while others had other explanations.

One evening during a heart-to-heart talk, Grace told me that some people back in Hawai'i were giving her a hard time. As they began hearing of Grace's plans to refuse the cut and kill approach, they didn't take it well. They had donated their leave time and hinted that she was squandering it. They didn't mind so much that she was using their sick time to spend a year on health. They minded that she didn't seem to want to live. These people liked and cared for Grace, and they were understandably entrenched in their Western beliefs: "You fight cancer by cutting it and zapping it. That's just how it's done. If you don't do that, you must have a death wish." A couple of these colleagues called Grace to let her know that they thought she was making a mistake. They tried to convince her. When Grace explained her approach, they became sad that she seemed unreasonable. I was appalled to learn this; these were people I knew. None of this was good for Grace. She was doing the bravest work ever — confronting her past and making all things right. What liberty! What peace! I screamed inside, *Why can't they just admire you?* Grace's story inspired me to look back on my own life and wonder what I had left unhealed. I've been leaning into processing the deaths, but my struggles for independence during motherhood and the loss of my job still stung.

"What did you say to them?"

"I didn't know what to say. I just listened. I think I just need to tell everyone, 'I need your support, not your challenge of my decision. Period.'"

For our remaining days together, our Taiwan adventure continued along the southeastern side of the island in Taitung and Hua Lian, where we met Grace's sister Josy and her family, then Grace and Josy's uncle and grandfather. I was thrilled to meet them. We toured organic farms, an archeological dig, a natural hot spring, Taroko Gorge, a Buddhist educational center, a Buddhist convent, a jade studio, a beach, and several parks. There were new experiences, inside jokes, and deep conversations at each turn.

At the conclusion of our adventure, Grace shared with me the top three things she had learned, and she asked for mine. These were Grace's lessons in her exact words:

1. I know more about a prince who lived in India more than 2,500 years ago than about anything in Taiwan history.
2. It is very interesting to see Taiwan from the eyes of a different culture. For example, I took it for granted that we do single-file, while Kelly questioned the relationship between single-file and finding inner peace.
3. I have a great family with very cool family members. I need to love them more and spend more time with them.

I learned numerous valuable life-long lessons that I continue to remind myself of, but I narrowed my list down to eleven to share with Grace. These were my top three.

1. Be aware of and enjoy the gifts of the present.
2. "Not thinking" is possible and valuable. There is a difference between heightened awareness – connecting to our senses, emotions, and thoughts in the present moment – which is good for our spirits, and thinking — and the ego-centric stories we tell ourselves about the past, future, and what's "really going on here." That kind of thinking can keep us from genuinely taking in our present surroundings.
3. I have ownership for the quality of my own life. *I* can change the quality of *my* relationships (all by myself). I'm

not stuck blaming others and waiting for them to change.
I can change me.

Just a few months after our grand adventure, in May
2012, at the one-year mark for her diagnosis, Grace went back to
the same surgeon she had seen with me in Hawai'i for a follow-
up mammogram. The tumor was still there, but no bigger — still
stage 1. Grace called to tell me. I was blown away.

Over the course of the next year Grace returned to
Honolulu and became more involved in a new age group
connected to her living philosophy. My visit with her came at a
pivotal moment for her as she was transitioning her belief system
from Buddhism toward new age. She enjoyed a book series
called *Seth Speaks*. On the surface, it seemed very unusual to me
— an energy personality named Seth spoke through a woman,
Jane Roberts's body, and she wrote books with Seth's messages.
Seth provides deep-cutting philosophical insights that Grace finds
to be practical perspectives on a daily basis.

I mentioned to Grace that I had worked with an energy
healer just two years earlier when my son was born, and she
wanted to look her up. She did. I was open to all of these ideas,
but I just didn't know if they were my own… yet. Many of the
Seth teachings that Grace shared with me made perfect sense. We
both agreed that it probably doesn't matter how the messages
arrive if the messages are valuable.

I deeply admire Grace. She is the one person in this world
who I think has *the* most integrity of anyone I've ever met —
hands down. She is exactly who she says she is, and backs it up
with difficult decisions. She's my hero on spiritual integrity,
communication skill, and holistic health. In some ways, she's
what I strive to be, but I doubt I could forgo Western medical
opinion when my life is on the line. I need more peace, love,
forgiveness, and patience in my life.

And, yes, I mean "she is." At this writing, Grace has
survived ten years since her diagnosis. She's only had a few
mammograms in that time, and intermittently has decided that
she doesn't really care to have any more. While she seems to me
to have transcended fear, she tells me, "Oh, I'm afraid." She sits
in it, feels it, and accepts that it is part of her.

Grace is wildly optimistic and adventurous. Since returning to her life in Honolulu, she's gone on snorkeling adventures, traveled to several new countries, and went on an Alaskan cruise with her mom. She was even awarded tenure by her department. As I'm writing this, she's in China with her mother traveling the "Silk Road." Her intentional zest for life reminds me of Miriam, but her desire to live authentically, not just into her future, but also into her past, I have never witnessed before.

Grace does not want to be approached with pity or judgement. Don't be sad for her. Don't have that look in your eyes that says, *Get legitimate treatment already!* Don't attempt to focus her mental energy on contemplating sickness. It's not the direction she's trying to go. But Grace is so gracious, she has contrived a way to deal with these well-meaning questions. In her head she translates these questions into statements "I'm thinking about you and care about you." That's much easier for her to respond to. She says, "Thanks so much for asking" in a heart-felt way because she knows that's what these folks really mean.

I continued to journal my reflections about my trip to Taiwan and my learnings from Grace, and work them into my own understanding of me.

May 30, 2016 Journal Entry
Both Rebecca and Grace lived with integrity — both struggled deeply to be exactly who they believed they were. But witnessing their paths taught me more about what my own integrity might look like should I fall ill. I'm not sure who I am, especially not now. I have no religion; I don't care to have one. I'm miserable in my job because I don't feel valued, but I'm not certain what I should be valued for. Faced with death, certainly I would not want to make decisions like Rebecca's. And though I aspired to have the integrity of Grace, I doubt that I could. I'm not even sure what I believe about health and life. I'll likely hit somewhere in the middle, making decisions more like Miriam or Nick. Even now, without illness, I know my actions don't match my beliefs

about myself. I say I care about social justice and that I reject racism and sexism, but I know those are deeply ingrained systems and values in each of us — including me. Do I do enough to resist the system and to effect change? I hope so. But to do that fully, I think I'd have to speak out more at work and risk losing my job. I may have already done that too much. My job already feels at risk. I say that consumerism and materialism are hurting our environment and even the sustainability of our economy, and yet I participate in these practices without much reflection. Grace and I both believe that we deserve love and patience from ourselves. I think she achieves it better. My awareness of my integrity seems to be satisfactory, but who I am exactly is still unknown.

Chapter 21

Journey

Four years after my visit with Grace in Taiwan my work life felt less and less rewarding. I had landed an administrator position at a college where I felt that I was undervalued and underutilized. I tried to "prove myself" and in doing so, my thoughts had become consumed with convincing others of my worth. I would sometimes make comments to knock others down in an effort to demonstrate my value. Unresolved resentment and rage were bubbling just below the surface of my interactions. I wasn't proud of who I was becoming. I began seeing a therapist aptly named Journey.

During one of my sessions with Journey, I was struck by how much of our time was consumed with me rehashing the same old thoughts, over and over. I grew tired and even resentful of how much brain space my work issues were taking. I remarked, "I want to talk about my life. That's the real thing. Let's step away from my work issues. Next time we meet, can we talk about my life? It's been a bumpy ride. I have been buffeted. I've experienced the deaths of too many peers, and I need to figure out what it all means."

Journey was interested, "Yes, that sounds like a great idea. It's kinda like you are dying right now."

"Oh, gosh, that's sounds about right," I said, and as I turned to head out, the truth of her comments set in. During my drive home I had the crashing feeling that Journey was more right than I initially assumed.

My thoughts flashed back to a conversation that I had nearly forgotten from four years earlier. My trip to Taiwan was in part motivated out of a desire to check-in on Grace, to truly see how she was doing. Through my experiences with Nick and Miriam, I felt I had become good at talking with people about cancer, and I wanted to be there for Grace if she'd let me. At the time of that trip, it had been ten months since I had seen her last and since she had received her breast cancer diagnosis. I had tried to keep in touch and to extend support from my Virginia home to hers in Taipei, but it felt strained. On FaceTime conversations I asked "How are you?" only to be met with "good" or "fine," even after my pleas for "No really, how *are* you with the cancer?" On this trip I was determined to be the confidante that I felt she needed. But the truth was rather the other way around, and I had no idea.

The evening after our day-long meditative hike in Taiwan, Grace took me to her favorite vegetarian restaurant. I filed through my mental rolodex of questions to find one that would get her to open up about the emotional challenges of having cancer. I found it. It was the same question I had felt too hesitant to ask Miriam. After our conversation steadied, there was a comfortable silence. We studied the room, our plates, and the air. Finally, I looked at her. It was time for my question.

"Grace, are you dying?" To my surprise she laughed at me. Grace threw her head back and laughed her raucous laugh. I didn't know what was so funny. Any fears I had that my question would be too challenging were gone, but I was unsure about where I stood in this moment.

"Yes!" She answered as soon as she gathered her breath again. She glared at me with a wise smirk, "and so are you!"

I am? Oh, yeah, right. Of course I am. "We are all dying." I get it.

Oh come on, Grace! Okay, okay I get it. You aren't having emotional challenges. At least not yet. I am. I am the one who is overwhelmed with confusion about what all this cancer stuff means. Not you.

"That's true," I replied. Although, I felt her answer still missed the point of my question. It didn't.

Nevertheless, I adjusted to be with her where I thought she was. And just like that, the deep truth and complexity of Grace's answer went right over my head. Four years later during my car ride home from my therapist's office, Grace's words hit me hard. I finally knew what Grace said was deeply true.

I am *dying. And not just metaphorically. What I'm experiencing is not a "kinda" death or just a career or identity death. But I truly am dying. We all are. I am.*

All this time I had wondered what I would do if I found out I was dying. All this time I've been envious in part of my dying friends because I admired what they had done to live authentic lives. They reprioritized life and lived into their priorities. The realization hit me hard and suddenly.

I don't have to wonder what I'd do. I'm doing it now. I can live an admirable life now.

Soon after this breakthrough I made a list of what dying people do, at least in my experience. I made a list of names, people who had been important to me. If I died soon, I'd want these people to know that I appreciated them and the influence I knew they had in my life. I got to work reaching out to them. I had deep conversations with my parents and shared my gratitude for each of them. I am grateful for my father's perseverance and unconditional love and my mother's bravery and commitment to learning. I wrote letters to several of my supervisors, deans, advisors, and mentors. I contacted Professors Jeff and Nancy to tell them their role in my path and to extend gratitude. All of them saw me, and I was so grateful to have experienced that in this lifetime.

I resigned from my job and reorganized my professional life. I volunteered for causes that I cared about. I took vacations. I wanted to go to the beach, so I took the kids and made a point to enjoy their company. I even took vacations by myself, retreats really. I made plans for bigger experiences that I wanted — like writing this book. I met with people who I had experienced as toxic to me and extended compassion and forgiveness for being just as human as me — and I also kept my distance. I created and defended explicit personal boundaries for what I would tolerate in my life. I dove into couples counseling with Dan to begin addressing the resentment I had been aiming at him for the normal challenges of co-parenting and the resulting loss of my career.

I asked myself: *If I knew my life would be short, what would I do differently? If I knew my life would be long, what would I do differently?* I attended to my answers and made intentional choices about how to spend my time and energy.

My therapist, Journey, often says, "When the student is ready, the teacher appears." Through my reflections with Journey, I can see the teachers in my life, but many of them have appeared to me through hindsight. Thank goodness for my life-long journaling habit, good memory, and a great therapist! I have been fortunate to know several amazing people who were going through the most challenging moments of their lives — family members, partners, friends, and coworkers. To witness these moments, and these teachers, has been instructive to my own life's journey.

Knowing and loving Chris pushed me to question my beliefs. From Maria, I learned to question my beliefs more critically and to sit with uncertainty. Knowing Maria invited me to be open to love beyond the boundaries of cultural expectation. From Shannon I learned to hold precious my own identity and boundaries, especially as I help others. I learned from the sudden and accidental losses of Chris and Shannon the reality of my own mortality. From Elizabeth, I learned that enduring love is when someone makes equal sacrifices to be with me that I make to be with them — to not give too much of myself away. Nick opened me to the idea that our relationships are not accidental; they are delivered to us. From Nick's wife, Elaine, I learned that to be genuinely known and loved is a gift, and perhaps it's a goal in life. From Miriam, I learned to be more comfortable with death, to not fear my emotions. She let me know that "real friends" are not necessarily the ones who could keep their emotions together and who would do favors for you. Rather real friends are the ones worth keeping, who have no emotional demands, who feed you spiritually rather than drain you. Also from Miriam, I learned what re-prioritizing life looks like, what it means to live honestly into your own expressed dreams and goals. From watching both Rebecca and my grandmother struggle and suffer with their beliefs in their final days, I concluded that certainty of religious belief can be damaging in the face of life's uncertainly.

From my early experiences with Danny's survival and my later experiences of witnessing Peyton's gender journey, I was reminded that I cannot control other people's lives or will to live. I learned that my sons are not really mine. They are both their own people, and they determine their own paths. It's the same for anyone really. I learned that we make the best decisions that we can, even in the face of limited information, that we are *all* doing the best we can. I have grown to understand and to let go. I learned that I am just lucky, and did nothing, absolutely nothing, to deserve knowing my sons. Danny's pre-birth situation led me to consider alternative paths to healing. It was my experience with Danny that initially opened me up to the possibilities of mindfulness, meditation, and seeing energy. I discovered that although I had felt let down by my religious traditions years earlier, I still did have a spiritual lens through which I craved to see something bigger going on in the world.

From Dan I have discovered my whole self. All parts of my life came together when I met Dan. He knew exactly who I was and loved all of me, not because of or in spite of it. I learned I could do the same. The trajectory of Danny's birth story was set to drive us apart, but we committed to honest and difficult conversations and that habit has paid off throughout our relationship. Through our co-parenting, once again, I was reminded of the dangers of giving myself away — of losing me. I learned there's an element of me that believes love means self-sacrifice; it's a big gift I give. I learned that my building resentment of Dan was a signal that I had reached the limit of what I could give away. And rather than blame him or run from the relationship, we worked on it honestly and openly. When I felt myself slipping away, I eventually realized that I was in control of that. I'm the one who has to work to get me back into my own life. I learned that the unjust cultural expectation that I, the mom, be the one to sacrifice my purpose to raise *our* kids, was too great of a force to project onto Dan alone. I am still learning what it means to accept and not resist this force…that neither I nor Dan alone can fight it…that accepting this struggle does not mean I need to comply and give myself entirely away to the service of my family. I am exploring what it means to accept unjust social forces, but to also live in opposition to them. And I learned that it was important to me that both Dan and I grew our awareness of this force so that we could critique it rather than become subject to it.

From challenging work situations in both Hawai'i and Virginia I learned that the most difficult people can be the most powerful teachers. I learned that validation of my own worth can only come from me. I was reminded that others don't make me feel any particular way; I do that. They are not that powerful; I am. I can decide how I will feel. I am not powerless to my feelings. I have choice. I am never stuck in any life situation. Forgiveness is key to letting go of the poison that my resentment feeds into my mind. Hurt people can hurt people. As my awareness grew, I saw how often I had judged others negatively due to my own struggles to feel valued. As I let that go, I saw that my love for others was bound up in my love for myself. Even hurt people are doing the best that they can. Love is the answer.

From Grace...from Grace I have learned the most. Watching Grace decide how to live with cancer showed me what living into values looks like. Her integrity taught me the fundamental purpose of having beliefs. Grace taught me how to listen deeply to myself, how to find my innermost self. She taught me that there is darkness in there, but, in her words, "What is the most personal is the most universal." Darkness is in everyone; it's what makes us human. I can and should make friends with my whole self and love me, then I will be able to love others. Grace taught me to have patience as I sit with my questions. Most importantly, Grace taught me that I am dying. The time to live into my life's priorities is now.

The more I name the teachers of my life, the wider the network spans until I consider that everyone can be a teacher, if only I would tune in to hear them. Everyone has value. Everyone. That death has seemed to surround me, my senses have been particularly piqued to lean in and listen and to make meaning of death events — which has eventually spilled over to how I perceive other life events as well. I have sought purpose in the people and events of my life.

Though I have learned all of this, I have also already known all of this.

At the one year mark of my therapy, Journey remarked "You look so different from when you came in here a year ago." "Really?" I was surprised. "How so?"

"Hmmm…well, maybe you don't *look* different, but you seem to *feel* different – the way you sit there now, and your energy. You have grown."

"I have learned a lot."

"What have you learned? How would you describe it?"

I was stumped. Every lesson I could think of in the past year I knew I would have been able to articulate the year earlier. "If my now me could tell my year-ago me the lessons that would be ahead, I would have said, 'Yeah, I already know that.'"

"You think so?"

"Yeah, I can't think of a way to articulate everything that I've learned in a way that it would feel like new information for my year-ago self. Maybe I haven't learned new lessons, just new places where they apply. I already knew of the fallacy of a meritocracy, but didn't realize that I still sought validation of my worth from that system. I already knew people project their issues onto others, but I didn't see that I was doing that too. I already knew I was mortal, but I didn't know what that would mean to my daily living. I think I know all of the same general life lessons as a year ago, but I've learned them more deeply."

I supposed this is one of life's paradoxes, to know and not know something at the same time. And just as I could see this pattern in my immediate past, I understood that it must also be true for my future. I have become more immersed in a Socratic mindset that all knowledge already exists deep inside each of us. A skillful teacher is one who can ask the right questions to help us find the answers that we already know. I have learned to become my own Socratic teacher. As burning questions come up for me, I have learned to reflect back, "What if I told you, you already know the answer? Look at your past life lessons and see which apply here?" The truth of life is in life itself, if we care to look closely enough.

I believe what Journey saw in me that day was the radiance of my authentic self. I have come to believe that authentic selves are actually kind of attractive, literally. When I am authentic, I feel at peace with me, in love with me, and who I allow myself to be. I identify and seek places where who I am is already valued, no more proving it. I increased my awareness of the performances that we all put on for each other to prove our worth, and I don't want to play anymore. I just *am* valuable, as are all others. When I am able to be fully me, I am calm and pleasant, and I compliment others. My face is relaxed. I love my clothes because I wear what speaks to me rather than trying to shape how others see me. I style my hair how I want, not in some "this looks professional" style. I eat and drink what I want, and release myself from what others might think about my choices. I spend my time how I want. I wake up when I want, and I slide into and out of events when I want. I show up where I want, and I feel entirely good and at peace. I'm also less likely to offend people since my insecurities and controlling behaviors of the past are shrinking. And I'm actually pretty attractive. I mean I must be, because I think I look awesome. I feel awesome and cool and worthy. So I must be.

As I slide into a room where I know the universe wants me, I *feel* the space and I can sense others' energy too. They look like me with their calm bodies and voices, their listening ears and loving hearts. Their faces are soft and they ooze love, and I love them back. They look attractive too, and I study their lips and their hair. I wonder what they are doing next week and when we can hang out again. Can I invite them over? Can we go to an event together?

In the old days, I was quick to shut down this feeling. I would worry. *I am bisexual. I can't get close to anyone. What if there's a line that gets crossed? I can't even get close to that line. I can't. I want to maintain my trustworthiness.* I stayed away from people who I was drawn to. I felt embarrassed to be drawn to others. I thought it was a bisexual thing, that others didn't feel how I felt, and that if I showed how "into" others I could get, I'd creep them out. I knew of friends who had same-gender close friends, but they were straight people, and I felt I couldn't do that. I had assumed those kinds of intimate friendships were not for me. Now, though, I know that my internalized bi-phobia feelings had blocked me from a larger network of omnipresent love throughout humanity.

Kate Bowler, author of *Everything Happens for a Reason*, describes in her book her struggle with the feeling that she got cancer for a reason, like a punishment from God. I don't think I've consciously thought that — never as a punishment or consequence. However, as my awareness rose, I saw that I had developed a sense that I was *supposed to* learn lessons from my life experiences, that there was some purpose in it. The magnet in Nancy's office introduced the idea that life was giving me lessons intentionally. Subconsciously, I wondered if my lack of learning caused more terrible events to happen. If I didn't hurry up and learn the life lesson, the trend of dying peers would continue. I even warned folks I dated, "Yeah, all my exes are dead, so maybe you don't want to break up with me." My experience at Pearl Harbor forever shook me from even the subconscious belief that death was about me, that some sinister force was punishing me (and my peers) for my limited awareness. And the years after that day taught me that there is not pure chaos in the world either. I began to notice if I wanted to move on to the next great awakening, there would always be learning opportunities readily available to me to embrace. If I pause in awareness, listen and reflect in any moment, great or small, I will gather valuable lessons. Some of those lessons will connect with one another to form awakenings to universal truths. The process of awakening can connect so profoundly that the events seem meant to be.

No, I don't believe that any of these events happened to me to teach me a lesson, but I do believe that life lessons are in these events just the same. Lessons are everywhere, especially in the most difficult of life circumstances. No amount or quality of my learning could control whether events will happen, they just do. And no, they are not *about* me, but the events of my life certainly are *for* me — just as the events of your life are *for* you as well.

Isn't this what spirituality is…about seeking meaning and purpose? That had been lost on me for too long. To obsess over whether events were presented intentionally or not rather missed the point. My life has always been better served when I can find meaning in whatever comes my way. Every moment of life is rich with lessons, if only we do the awareness and reflection work to seek these lessons and to accept them. Difficult moments are for experiencing fully: sitting comfortably in the center of them, soaking in the moment, for they hold the truth of life. This is my journey.

Epilogue

While this book was in the process of being published, I learned that on Sunday morning, May 7, 2023, Grace passed away in her home city of Taipei, Taiwan. Her flowers are buried on the Yangming mountain top where she once whispered in my ear, "Be one with the bowl." She told me there, "This cancer has given me a beautiful struggle. I'm so grateful for this opportunity to be genuine, discover, and forgive." In a tribute released by her employer, one friend was quoted calling Grace, "our no nonsense, direct warrior of life" and, indeed, she was this for me and anyone who knew her. The same friend posed this challenge, "to celebrate her, may we live our lives to the fullest every day and love our neighbors, families, and friends," may it be so.

Grace's sister posted this request on Grace's social media accout, "Ask friends to bless her, she will know."

Acknowledgements

I've been telling versions of these stories in bits and pieces whenever they seem to come up in conversations with friends. Repeatedly folks would respond with, "Whoa, really? You should write a book." And that just seemed absurd. *It's my life, it's not a book. There's no plot.*

On precisely my 44th birthday it finally occurred to me how I could write this story. Upon reflection, death and loss were the obvious themes and how I viewed those events had clear pivot points – they'd make nice plot points. So I began to write with the hopes that I would be done by my 45th birthday. But that didn't happen. All told, it took me six years to write this book. It started with 15 minutes of writing per day, I exploited my bad habit of phone surfing at bedtime by turning it into productive writing time. I'd write an email to myself of a story that I knew would go somewhere in the manuscript. Then in the morning, I could cut and paste it into my outline. That was the first 50 pages. After that I sought personal writing retreats away from home: Lake Anna State Park, "The Porches" in Nelson County, Berkley Springs, Richmond Hill, Cranaleith Spiritual Center, Vass Courage and Renewal retreat, and Kirkridge Retreat Center. And when the Covid pandemic came, I retreated to my mother's house. I have grown, not just from experiencing or reflecting on my life, but from the act of writing it all down. I didn't expect to feel all of those same old emotions as I retold the details of the hardest parts of my life, but I did. I cried countless times over these pages, again and again as I reread drafts.

I am grateful for my family – my husband and two sons – for allowing me the "guilt-free" time and space to explore my own story so deeply. In many ways, I did this as a gift to them. I am grateful for my mother and father for their support and their modeling of life-long personal growth. I am thankful for my skillful editor, Ed Cyzewski, who somehow magically read 412 pages of my disjointed stories and found this 200-page book in there somewhere. I am thankful for early readers Anne Merrill, Rachel Giunta, Kate Tweedy, Grace Lin, Chael Wright-Isak, Ann Zweckbronner, Maren Larson, Beth Faivre, and Rhonda Toussaint. Most certainly this book would not be possible without the support of these loving humans.

About the Author

Kelly Carter Merrill is a professor of communication studies and nonprofit studies in central Virginia. She is a consultant for Gray Areas Consulting where she specializes in facilitating difficult conversations about community building, trauma healing, diversity and inclusion, self-discovery, and leadership for organizations, community groups, work places, and small nonprofits. Kelly blogs at GrayAreas.org.

Made in the USA
Middletown, DE
02 November 2024